PRAISE FOR *WHO ARE YOU & WHAT HAVE YOU DONE WITH MY KID?*

"Dr. Craig's brilliant 'tween' parenting guide takes the guesswork out of how parents can cultivate enduring emotional connections with their evolving preteen, while also teaching parents about the psychological foundations of human bonding and child development, and how to mindfully practice self-compassion along the way."

—ANDRE BUREY, MD, CHILD AND ADOLESCENT PSYCHIATRIST,
ON STAFF AT SILVER HILL HOSPITAL

"Dr. Craig is one of my favorite experts! She always brings joy and a depth of research to her interactions, and every mom (who I know) in town seeks her out for advice and encouragement. Here, she masterfully integrates knowledge, action, and love to help us in our families as we weave our lives together with our kids. I wish this book had been available to me when my boys were tweens!"

—BRANDI DRAKE, REV. AT NOROTON PRESBYTERIAN CHURCH,
DARIEN, CONNECTICUT

"Dr. Craig's expertise in family therapy and experience with her own faith make a powerful combination in this book. She will guide you in building a loving relationship with your tween, so that they will know that you see them, you want to know them, you are there for them, and that you will keep them safe."

—DIANE ROTH, REV. AT GRACE LUTHERAN CHURCH,
CONROE, TEXAS

"Wow, this is a phenomenal read, very inspiring, and full of empowering information about establishing a healthy emotional connection with tweens as they work through their life experiences. I warmly encourage every helping professional to purchase this book to learn about the importance of establishing a healthy emotional connection with their children as early as possible to enable them to have successful personal and relational experiences."

—DR. GARRETT INGRAM, PHD, MFT-I, OFFICE OF SPECIAL INVESTIGATIONS,
ADMINISTRATION FOR CHILDREN'S SERVICES, NEW YORK CITY

WHO ARE YOU & WHAT HAVE YOU DONE WITH MY KID?

CONNECT WITH YOUR TWEEN
WHILE THEY ARE STILL LISTENING

AMANDA CRAIG, PHD, LMFT

New York • Nashville

Worthy
Hachette Book Group
1290 Avenue of the Americas, New York, NY 10104
worthypublishing.com
twitter.com/worthypub

First Edition: September 2022

Worthy is a division of Hachette Book Group, Inc. The Worthy name and logo are trademarks of Hachette Book Group, Inc.

The publisher is not responsible for websites (or their content) that are not owned by the publisher.

The Hachette Speakers Bureau provides a wide range of authors for speaking events. To find out more, go to www.hachettespeakersbureau.com or call (866) 376-6591.

Library of Congress Cataloging-in-Publication Data
Names: Craig, Amanda (Family therapist), author.
Title: Who are you & what have you done with my kid? : connect with your
    tween while they are still listening / Amanda Craig, PhD, LMFT.
Other titles: Who are you and what have you done with my kid?
Description: New York, NY : Worthy, [2022]
Identifiers: LCCN 2022010852 | ISBN 9781546003083 (hardcover) | ISBN
    9781546003106 (ebook)
Subjects: LCSH: Parent and teenager. | Parenting. | Interpersonal
    relations.
Classification: LCC HQ799.15 .C69 2022 | DDC 306.874--dc23/eng/20220404
LC record available at https://lccn.loc.gov/2022010852

ISBNs: 9781546003083 (hardcover), 9781546003106 (ebook)

Printed in the United States of America

LSC-C

Printing 1, 2022

For my sister Val

CONTENTS

SECTION TWO: INTRODUCTION
Your Toolbox: How to Use What You've Learned · 159

Part Six: I See You · 163

Part Seven: I Want to Know You · 179

Part Eight: I Am Here for You · 219

Part Nine: I Will Keep You Safe · 241

Conclusion: On the Side of Us · 267

WHO ARE YOU
& WHAT HAVE
YOU DONE WITH
MY KID?

SECTION ONE
INTRODUCTION

BeTween Us:
The Future Is Now

So you have a tween…or perhaps you know one. Whatever your reason for picking up this book, I welcome you to this dive into the puzzle that is our nine- to twelve-year-olds. It's crazy-making as they move from the calm of young elementary school through the mayhem of middle school. But there are reasons why and ways to navigate it, and we will cover it all together.

Is it a rewarding time? Yes! But it can cost us—emotionally, physically, and spiritually. There's so much going on! For our tweens, it's a complex stretch tied to profound emotional, physiological, and neurological development with serious ramifications for their future—as teens and then as adults.

So often parents arrive at the tween years with a whoa-something's-happening-here sense of the change before them. And they're right. Something *is* happening…a lot, in fact. But rather than doing anything about it, we park in uncertainty, unsure about this tween in our midst—sometimes a stranger, but still that child we have always known—whiny and complaining but also laughing at silly jokes, cuddling, and wanting to be around us. So we don't think much about it, and instead we move from focusing on the academics and social concerns of elementary school straight to worries about safety, drugs, sex, and the rebellious behavioral issues of the teen years. We miss the tremendous parenting opportunities before us when our kids are tweens.

We don't want to just survive the tween years. We want to be proactive in our parenting. This is a time for *prevention* parenting, for shaping the choices our tweens will make as they move into adolescence. By the teen years, it's all about *intervention*, and the opportunity has passed us by.

And there's so much we can do!

So how do we keep our kids close while cultivating the confidence they'll need to grow up? How do we navigate the inevitable dips, divides, and potholes? Where do we find the strength, calm, self-awareness, and wisdom that amount to a path forward?

Surprisingly, there is very little accessible tween-focused parenting information available and certainly nothing that links emotional connection—the cornerstone of it all—with what is happening in the tween brain and what we must know about ourselves to lay a solid foundation for the teenage years and beyond. There is even less that ties the science of this to the strength and wisdom available to all of us, secular and non-secular, in our faith teachings. Parents need a blueprint, something more than tactics and strategies, something deeper than that, something that will actually work.

While intentionally written for the faith-curious and spiritual as well as the "faith-full," this book is driven by *my* faith. The initial draft poured from me, a calling to give parents the information and tools they need to create healthy relationships with their tween, head off problems before they happen, and address them when they do. It presents the wisdom found in faith teachings in combination with what we know from the fields of neuroscience and family therapy, specifically Emotionally Focused Therapy (EFT)—a therapeutic approach centered on emotional connection (and the backbone of my practice)—and applies them to parenting during the middle school years in a way that is accessible to the general public. After all, when eyes, minds, and hearts are open to it, it is easy to see that therapy is, in fact, a convergence of science and spirituality, beginning with the emotional connection modeled in our faith teachings and continuing through the spirit that lives in each of us.

Clinical psychologist Sue Johnson, the co-founder of EFT, points out that creating connections is hardwired into us. It is the lead element in our most ancient code of survival. We are *meant* to be in relationship with one another. We are *meant* to be in relationship with our tween. But it takes work, intention, commitment, and knowledge. The good news is, when our kids are tweens, we still have a "seat at the table" with them, a chance to teach, to shape, and to help them develop the life skills needed to explore the world around them, before our "chair" is pushed away during the teen years.

In my early twenties, just after I finished my master's degree in counseling psychology, my younger sister Valantina was murdered. She was eighteen years old. I was haunted by questions of what our family and I could have done differently to prevent the choices she made that inadvertently led to this tragedy. It fueled what was already a natural drive to focus on family therapy—observing and understanding family systems and the dynamics between family members. I was so intensely curious about parenting practices and the far-ranging effects of connected and conflictual or distant family relationships that I went back to school and earned a PhD in family psychology. Simultaneously, my faith strengthened, and I leaned into that strength to get through that terrible time. It has remained my foundation since.

I fell in love with understanding how family members impact the feelings of one another—in ways good and bad—and how patterns of behavior in families are generationally formed, always in the background of our thoughts, feelings, and actions. Additionally, I was drawn to the impact of different types of connection within families and how they affect people in adulthood.

My passion for family systems is informed by more than twenty years of clinical experience in family therapy, which was a relatively new therapeutic area when I entered the field. I was interested in how faith teachings could help change toxic patterns and move families toward more positive relationships. Having counseled thousands of family members—couples, blended families, those co-parenting, siblings, children, teens, and tweens—I've viewed family dynamics from every angle, including as a parent of a tween myself, and have come away with a deep understanding of the opportunities to improve tween parenting practices. It is from these experiences that I've selected a combination of case studies from my practice and experiences with my own tween for the book. Together, they create a personal, approachable context for the knowledge I share—the unique opportunities and challenges in raising a tween as well as how to navigate the inevitable conflicts.

It's all about emotional connection, and it is particularly important now as anxiety, mental illness, and lack of resilience continue to plague our young people earlier and more severely, impacting their psychological and physical health now and far into their future—and especially in the wake of the COVID-19 pandemic. It doesn't have to be that way. Welcome to *Who Are You & What Have You Done with My Kid?*

PART ONE

Love Wins

Emotional Connection: The Secret to Building a Strong Relationship with Your Tween

"Love has an immense ability to help heal the devastating wounds that life sometimes deals us. Love also enhances our sense of connection to the larger world. Loving responsiveness is the foundation of a truly compassionate, civilized society."

—SUE JOHNSON, PHD, CLINICAL PSYCHOLOGIST AND FOUNDER OF EMOTIONALLY FOCUSED THERAPY (EFT)

"(Love) always protects, always trusts, always hopes, always perseveres."

—1 CORINTHIANS 13:7 NIV

f you have a tween, you probably know this (all too well): Tweens are nine- to twelve-year-old, fifth- through eighth-grade, cell phone–toting, beginner makeup–wearing, fashionista, TikTok-creating, YouTube-watching conundrums. They morph before our eyes from affectionate and silly fourth graders to hieroglyphic souls, a mystery of contradicting behaviors that can confound even the wisest of parents, testing our patience and fortitude. One minute, we see the adult in them starting to form: They make their bed, brush their teeth, lay out their clothes, take responsibility,

TWEEN BEHAVIORS: THE ADULT THEY'RE BECOMING, THE CHILD THEY STILL ARE

Adult Behaviors We Start to See	Child Behaviors Still Present
Laying out clothes for the next day	Little interest in clothes beyond comfort
Organizing schoolwork and schedule	Trouble putting words to needs, telling time, and knowing their schedule
Sharing thoughts and feelings	Irrational, temper tantrums, whining, or clinging
Decorating their room	More interested in toys than room decor
Making plans with friends without parental involvement	Having disagreements or being overwhelmed by friendship
Going out with friends without adult supervision	May get scared during a sleepover at a friend's house
Having ideas about social trends; discussing politics	Taking things they hear as facts
Understanding the value of a dollar	Little thought about money; focused on "wanting what they want" now
Following step-by-step instructions (in recipes, model making, etc.)	Disorganized, impulsive
Remembering to do chores (no, this does not include personal hygiene)	Chores? What chores?

and express themselves with emerging maturity. The next, they're whining, crying, clinging, or throwing a tantrum like a small child. It's the whiplash start of the push-and-pull relationship with us that will last through their teens.

The tween years are a crossroads in our parenting journey. I'm there too. (I also have a tween.) It's worth every effort we can possibly make to get it right with our child. And we can! No matter how they may behave, they want us to *know* them; they want us to *care* about their opinions; they want to *play* with us. They're trying to get us to *see* them. They *want* a bond with us. It's called **emotional connection.** Establishing and maintaining it is the key to navigating the conundrum that is our tween.

It's not just about creating peace in our home (as important as this is), it's about using *everything* available to us during the tween years (and there is a lot) to *grow close* to our kids, because **the tween we have today will become the teenager in our home tomorrow and the adult down the road…and the relationship we build now will last a lifetime.** What's more, the closer the bond we have with our kids now, the better we will be able to set them on a course to the life we dream for them.

As parents, we talk about what to do and what not to do in how we raise our tweens as they graduate from playdates to the more independent "just hanging." Some may approach parenting intellectually and intentionally with strategies and tactics. Other parents may try to be pals, or go to the opposite extreme, enforcing strict boundaries as they push their kids to be the best versions of themselves. Perhaps some of us try to protect our child and take it too far, or we roll into each day hanging on for dear life as we try to balance the many demands on our time. Or maybe we just react, for reasons we'll come to understand better in the following chapters. Most of us are a combination of all of the above. When we drive from these parenting strategies, we often lose, because without emotional connection with our tween, we can't really get anywhere. It's why we can *do* all the right things with our tween and still feel stuck.

It's like this: If our relationship with our tween is a house we are building, emotional connection serves as the studs and beams that hold it together.

THE EMOTIONALLY CONNECTED TWEEN

Emotionally Connected Tween	Emotionally Disconnected Tween
Follows rules	Doesn't understand/mind the rules; can't follow what they don't get
Feels part of family	Feels isolated
More apt to resist peer pressure	Has trouble finding their voice, so harder to resist peer pressure
A better friend, teammate	Suspicious of the intentions of others
Open-minded, more apt to try new things	Avoids new experiences
Shares thoughts and feelings; asks for help	Guarded about what they will share
Makes up after an argument	Ignores, blames, holds a grudge
Learning to be self-aware, empathetic	Insecure about their feelings and how to express them
Resilient	Shut down

That's why everything I say and do with the parents and tweens I counsel (and with my own tween) ties back to creating emotional connection.

With emotional connection, we have trust and a way forward with our tween; we can find out who they are and discover what they've done with the kid we always knew. They register us as part of their team, able to keep them safe in a world that can be unpredictable and, at times, downright scary. To them, we are a place of stability. They see us as someone who wants to listen to their thoughts and stories, and they feel comfortable sharing with us. They know that when things are tough, we will sit with them in their distress, hear their perspective, and empathize with their struggle.

They feel understood and supported. Emotional connection preserves order in the family, reinforces love, and builds respect among family members.

When a strong emotional connection exists, our tween is more apt to follow rules, make up after an argument, and ask for help. They trust our wisdom and how we parent them. We become their guiding light. When we are emotionally connected, we can also have the hard conversations, set boundaries, enforce the rules, and teach the lessons that give our tween the courage and character to be resilient and thrive. They might not always like where we steer them, but they understand it comes from a good place and ultimately has a good outcome for them.

When emotional connection is absent, it's going to be a tough go, pretty much no matter what: The way we communicate love and our desire to be close gets lost in translation. Our tween may think we don't care about what is important to them and register our behavior as something they can't trust, something with hidden messages or intentional meanness. They may feel alone, hurt, and angry and see us as unreliable. They may not respect us, listen to us, or talk openly to us. They may rebel against rules, yell, and cry, latch on to things they don't like and harp on them obsessively, or they may shut down, avoiding conversation and family time. All of this is a protest against the disconnection they feel.

When the inevitable conflicts appear, we may try different approaches: tough love, enabling, engaging, explaining, hands-off, ignoring, punishment, withholding love, hovering, offering more love, nagging, and yelling. We may talk to friends, read books, go to support groups, speak to therapists, listen to podcasts, attempting anything and everything to keep our children safe, only to hit a wall, which leaves us feeling defeated, frustrated, and unsure how to change the dynamic. These are holes only emotional connection can fill.

CHAPTER ONE

THE FOUR PILLARS OF EMOTIONAL CONNECTION

Many of us are parenting our kids to be "happy" or "successful." We think we're connecting emotionally but we're not. Tween parenting is not about doing the "right" thing.

It is about showing up to engage with our child from a place of emotional connection in which we communicate:

- I see you.
- I want to know you.
- I am here for you.
- I will keep you safe.

Here's what I mean.

I See You

When our tween feels seen by us at home, they feel we truly care for them. They may be different from us or from what we think best serves them, but when we see them for who they really are, and honor it rather than discourage it, they start to feel that they matter and their voice matters.

This translates into stronger self-worth and confidence to share their thoughts.

It comes from being heard rather than being dismissed, told they are wrong, or not given the chance to talk. This gives our tween the opportunity to practice different voices: sharing things that are difficult to talk about, identifying and describing their emotions, and telling us when they are not happy with us or someone else. Sometimes they may not make sense or be quite right in what they are saying or doing, but when we give them space to talk or do things on their own, they pick up on how they sound and discern whether they want to change their views or actions: They grow in how they communicate about the world.

They develop the confidence to talk to adults, coaches, teachers, and peers. They assume they will be seen and heard—that what they say matters, because that is what they have practiced at home. They speak from a stance of "let me share something" rather than "give me attention."

They are able to show up as a better teammate, classmate, sibling, and friend. They begin to take on the world with an open mind, pushing themselves outside their comfort zone, getting up when they fall down, and engaging with new people, places, and things with curiosity. Simple acts such as raising their hand with a question in class are more attainable to them. They are more apt to say no to a peer doing something they don't agree with because they have the words and emerging self-knowledge to do it, and they take responsibility when they misbehave.

I Want to Know You

Whether they know it consciously or not, our tween is looking for people who will understand them, accept them, and help them make sense of what they are going through...and it is a lot, thanks to the massive neurological changes happening inside their brains. (Fasten your seat belt. We'll get to that in Part Two: It's Not You, It's Neuroscience.) Their emotions can be extreme, and they are not yet equipped to put words to them or turn down the heat when those emotions get too big.

Happily, at this point in their lives, the people tweens look to most are still adults, namely us! When we show our tween that we want to go deeper, to *really* listen and know them, they will share their thoughts and ideas, talk about their emotions and what they are experiencing day to day. Showing our tween *I want to know you* teaches them self-awareness and empathy while improving their communication and coping skills as well as their decision-making ability. It makes them a better friend: As they feel our empathy, they learn to show it to others.

To know our tween is to take "seeing" them to a whole new, deeper level. And when we go deeper with our tween, allowing them to share what they view as their wins, understanding their humor and their unique take on life, not only do we build emotional connection, we also reinforce the joy of this crazy parenting wheel we've jumped on and create a lasting relationship with our tween.

I Am Here for You

It's no secret: When we're part of something bigger than ourselves—like a supportive group with which we are fully connected—we feel tremendous security. It's especially true with tweens when we create an emotionally close family…by playing together, working together, learning from one another, being present for one another, and spending time together. Win, lose, or draw, they know there's a team to celebrate with them, put things in perspective, and help them rebalance their world when it feels out of whack. They know if they crash and burn, we will pick them up, dust them off, and keep moving forward with them. We build a safe place for failure, falling, and mistakes. And when tweens feel we have their back unconditionally, they feel loved; they feel "good enough."

It gives our tween the foundation from which to take healthy risks and conquer the fears and insecurities so prevalent at this age. It gives them the courage to sign up for an after-school class, walk into a room where they may not know anyone, and stand up to bullies, even when it means standing against their peers.

When I was eleven years old, I took gymnastics. To this day, I remember a group of siblings who formed their own team. Their mom was their coach. I was captivated…a family big enough to make a team?! Coached by a parent?! As one of just two siblings, I recall thinking how fun it would be to have so many brothers and sisters all doing the same thing together. I imagined they never fought but rather cartwheeled and flipped through their days together, ever growing in their skills as the older kids helped the younger ones, proud parents watching them play and work together. Okay, so there was definitely some childhood fantasizing going on here but what I was picking up on was the *I am here for you* pillar of emotional connection…the support and confidence kids feel in being part of something bigger than themselves, what it's like in a family with common goals and values; a family that works together, helps each other, learns from one another, has fun and plays together.

I Will Keep You Safe

To create fully formed emotional connection with our tween, we *must* set boundaries. Boundaries tell our tween we are committed to their safety, that we are connected to them through the concern that drives our rulemaking. They offer our tween a push pin of sorts, indicating that beyond a certain point, there will be danger. They give our tween the chance to feel the discomfort, guilt, and regret that comes with crossing the lines we set. Conversely, when they obey the rules, they have the opportunity to feel protected by us. Boundaries are also how our tween learns about discipline and delaying gratification.

While boundaries are a key part of emotional connection, I cannot tell you how often I see parents go straight to them without first establishing *I see you, I want to know you,* and *I am here for you.* They will fight this tooth and nail then wonder why there's such a disconnect with their tween.

For boundaries to become the connector they can be, our tween must feel seen, known, and part of something bigger than themselves. Hard conversations demand relationship first. This is essential, and you will hear it again, because when our tween feels a strong bond with us, they will trust our boundaries rather than view them as a scheme to control them.

The Pillars of Emotional Connection
I see you.
I want to know you.
I am here for you.
I will keep you safe.

CHAPTER TWO

EMOTIONAL CONNECTION: ORIGIN AND IMPACT

At its core, emotional connection is about love, the unconditional kind we find in faith…the kind that gives us the inner confidence to stand up for ourselves and do what's right, to go after our dreams, to take risks. It powers our lives with meaning, gratitude, and authenticity. It connects us with others and makes us strong, empathetic, and giving. When we love ourselves, we love others. It's why so much of what we learn in our faith communities returns endlessly to the recurring theme of love and why it is so critical to the relationship we are able to build with our tween. Science concurs.

Emotional connection takes place in our nervous system. Our nervous system is like the operating system of a computer, unseen but powering all activity. It hums along in the background of our lives—a dense web of overlapping activity beyond our conscious thinking, shaping our relationships in ways we never imagined.

At the top level, the nervous system consists of the somatic and autonomic systems. (Hang in there with me on all this science—it is important as it shows that emotional connection is not simply a concept out of a church or therapist's office. It's real, it's physical…and it's a big deal.) The somatic nervous system is the boss of our voluntary response to external stimuli. The autonomic nervous system heads up our involuntary body functions—our heartbeat, breathing, digestion, etc., but also, interestingly, how we react viscerally to things…for example, the emotions we feel. *It is where nearly everything we'll cover in this book lives.*

The autonomic nervous system is further broken out into two camps: the sympathetic system and the parasympathetic system. When we feel calm and rested, the parasympathetic system is in charge. All is well. We're open and responsive.

The sympathetic system takes over when we are nervous or afraid—of a test, a bully, of being left out, or when a relationship feels unsafe…any situation that makes us want to run for the hills or dig in our heels, fists up. It's where that fight-or-flight impulse exists within us.

What's more, the sympathetic and parasympathetic systems have a direct line to the rest of our bodies. When the parasympathetic system is driving the bus, things are quiet throughout our body. However, when we're nervous or afraid, the sympathetic system is on an internal loud-speaker telling our body to be on alert:

- Our hearts beat faster.
- Our liver stimulates a sugar release to fuel the increased focus and energy it thinks we will need.
- Our lungs expand, sending oxygen through our bloodstream in preparation for the exertion it expects to come.
- Our eyes widen or pupils dilate.
- Our digestive system hits pause as our sympathetic nervous system reserves energy for survival rather than basic functions.

…and what the sympathetic system starts, our hormones sustain. That's why it can be so hard to simply end an argument with our tween. Once revved up, the body isn't so keen to let it all go.

AUTOMATIC NERVOUS SYSTEM

Sympathetic "Fight or Flight"

Parasympathetic "Rest and Digest"

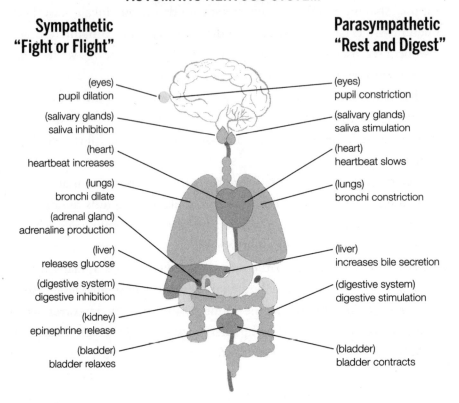

(eyes)
pupil dilation

(eyes)
pupil constriction

(salivary glands)
saliva inhibition

(salivary glands)
saliva stimulation

(heart)
heartbeat increases

(heart)
heartbeat slows

(lungs)
bronchi dilate

(lungs)
bronchi constriction

(adrenal gland)
adrenaline production

(liver)
releases glucose

(liver)
increases bile secretion

(digestive system)
digestive inhibition

(digestive system)
digestive stimulation

(kidney)
epinephrine release

(bladder)
bladder relaxes

(bladder)
bladder contracts

Parts of the body impacted by the parasympathetic and sympathetic systems and the physical responses associated with each

Emotional connection comes through the parasympathetic nervous system. That's why we feel it throughout our body. On the flip side, when we disconnect emotionally, our sympathetic nervous system comes online, effectively shouting "Danger!" and sending the distress signals that set off all those fight-or-flight physical responses. That's right: When we feel distant from the people closest to us, we activate our stress response system. The same goes for tweens when they feel separated from us. Not surprisingly, all of this has a profound impact on our physical and mental health as well as our response to nearly everything.

According to research compiled by *The Harvard Review* and the National Institutes of Health, when we have strong relationships with our partner and our children (like emotional connection), we are happier and healthier. We are composed, open, easier to be close to. We handle stress better, have more energy, are more apt to take healthy risks and live longer. It is our parasympathetic system at work. When our relationships are broken, things go in the opposite direction.

Further confounding the whole equation, we attach feelings to the emotions that come from the experiences that activate our sympathetic and parasympathetic systems. Feelings are the words we assign to emotions based on our experiences, beliefs, memories, thoughts, and values. If we wanted, we could measure the physical changes caused by emotions in our nervous system through things such as an electrocardiogram (EKG), an electroencephalogram (EEG), or by watching changes in facial expression, posture, or body language. Conversely, if we wanted to measure feelings, we would have to use self-reporting tools such as interviews or questionnaires.

When we are happy, relaxed, and/or joyful, we are what we call in my field regulated. Our nervous system is calm. We feel good about ourselves and close in our relationships. We are emotionally connected. We have more energy and focus. Shame, disappointment, and the weight they carry with them have left the building. All is right in the world.

On the other hand, when we feel discomfort, nervous, and/or frustrated, our thoughts start to cloud, our behaviors change toward ourselves and others, we are dysregulated. Our nervous system is on alert. Maybe we are guarded. Perhaps we feel the danger of approaching conflict and become defensive, combative, or withdrawn. Whether we fight or flee, it will almost always leave us feeling defeated, sad, taken advantage of, or guilty. We are emotionally disconnected.

Emotions drive the patterns of behavior we see in ourselves and our tween, sparking what can seem like impulsive reactions—positive and negative. These are feelings on full display. They are subjective, instinctual, and they happen fast, which is why it is difficult to simply change a response on command. To change any behavior, we must change our emotions first. And to do that, we need emotional connection. (If you're feeling overwhelmed, not to worry: We'll cover all this in much greater depth as we move through the coming chapters.)

CHAPTER THREE

PARENTING WITH EMOTIONAL CONNECTION

Parenting with emotional connection is a home run at any stage. Why is it particularly important during the tween years? With all the changes our tween is experiencing in their brain, in friendships, and at school, they need reassurance that they are seen and understood, part of a safe community. They crave the feedback that they are "good" and doing life "right," and if not, we are there to help them navigate the stormy waters. When they feel emotional connection with us, they feel good about themselves.

Emotional connection with our tween sets the stage for how they will grasp and cope with their emotions, understand others, experience close relationships, and express empathy and compassion. Emotional connection also provides the foundation from which our tween starts to become independent, try new things—even when they feel difficult—and persevere through obstacles as they move into their teen years and beyond. It's because they feel safe *inside* the home that they are compelled to take healthy risks *outside* of it.

Even more importantly, if our tween feels emotionally connected with us, they will be more apt to confide their secrets, hurts, fears, and vulnerabilities in their teen years when the stakes are higher. They will take what we say and do during the teen years more seriously because they've learned to trust that our intentions are in their best interest. And what they practice during their teens years will build their resilience and ability to navigate tough situations. This gives them a solid base from which to launch into early adulthood both in the goals they set and the relationships they pursue.

So if emotional connection is the structure for building our relationship with our tween, why is it so often overlooked or trivialized? Well, for starters, our culture doesn't value it. Though it may have been unconsciously modeled for us in our own upbringing (or not), we aren't getting the message in our day-to-day lives that it exists and that it's important to take the time to really tune in to the people who matter to us, especially our kids and particularly our tweens.

I think back to *Growing Pains*, a popular sitcom that aired from 1985 to 1992. It won multiple Primetime Emmy Awards and was a perennial nominee for a slew of other honors. It was one of the hottest shows on TV. The actors modeled emotional connection. The featured family smiled at one another. They laughed at one another's jokes. They sat on the couch together.

TikTok's not showing us that. YouTube's not showing us that. Video games aren't showing us that. Reality TV for sure isn't showing us that. We see it in our faith communities, but they are so often put on the back burner of our busy lives. So where are we learning to sit down and enjoy dinner together or just be with one another? It's the last thing on our priority list—a sort of "Never mind that…"

"I have to work late."

"I have to go to this volunteer thing."

"I have sports."

"I have homework."

We think, *Of course these things take precedence. We're all trying to succeed and this is as it should be!*

In reality, they are replacing time with our tween, the time needed to emotionally connect—which has far greater influence on long-term success than grades!

The other very common phenomenon I see is when we do make time for our tween, we're only fractionally there. I just had a client talking about this. She said she gets so strung out by her day at work that when she does sit down with her child to read a book or listen to their violin practice, she's just going through the motions rather than truly dropping into the experience and feeling the music, hearing her tween's mastery of a difficult passage, or reading the book with energy and personality. Compounding this is the amount of time both parents and tweens spend on electronics: We are endlessly preoccupied with the latest thing on our screen, texts, and email; distracted by beeps and reminders; and limited by our short attention spans, conditioned as we are to digest information in increments of thirty seconds (or less).

And if there's a problem, we go to fix it, quickly and efficiently. We're coming from the right place: As parents, we have a caregiving system built in. We naturally love our children and want what is best for them. It is the spirit within us at work. We don't want our tween to hurt so we think: *Let me get rid of that for you.* But in the process we leave our tween in their pain. Because while we may have fixed the problem, if we haven't stopped to hear them out, to understand what's really going on and comfort them, they're still hurting. It takes time and focus to process the hurt with our tween, to sit with them through the sadness and then help them find answers. But when we do this (rather than provide the answers), we show we care, that we understand their feelings, that we are there for them: We build emotional connection.

Co-parenting to Emotionally Connect

While a loving relationship may end between two adults, it doesn't end for the children. Divorce is an adult solution to an adult problem. Divorce doesn't necessarily provide a solution for a child. *How* we co-parent in divorce is what matters to our tween. Even if the other parent no longer lives in the same house with us, we must support each other, no matter how deep our differences may be. Tweens notice and will attach meaning to our relationship and apply it to how they feel about themselves and us.

We can emotionally connect with our tween by showing respect for their other parent. Remember, both parents play a significant role in a tween's life and in their understanding of themselves. Parents model how tweens see themselves, assert their needs, push the envelope, and strive in what matters to them. Parents also model the type of partner a tween will seek/gravitate toward, how they will treat their partner and contribute to the family they create.

To dump on the other parent criticizes the part of our tween that identifies with that parent. They might stop liking that part of themselves, think *we* don't like a part of them, get angry at the parent for having the part we disparage, or pull away from us for speaking negatively about it.

If co-parents fight or disagree and a tween witnesses it, it's okay, if they see a resolution afterward. They must feel they are in a safe, stable family, regardless how traditional or non-traditional it may be. Arguments are a normal part of relationships. When they occur, we must share feelings and thoughts instead of blame. We must express needs, accept the other person, and reach a solution. A tween will learn that an argument is not the end of the world. They will learn how to fight fairly, handle conflict, and make amends rather than suppress emotions, not communicate or scream to get a point across—unhealthy alternatives to say the least! Ironically, being able to disagree and make up means that emotional connection is fully present in the relationship.

The Stage Is Set

Everyone longs to be close, even when they push away. It is a God-given thing. Likewise, our tween craves closeness with us—emotional connection, even when they act like it's the last thing they want, and even though they have no idea just how badly they need it to move into the rest of their lives. They just want it. And that's such good news for us: Our stage is set! We need merely to act. Our tween is waiting for us. Love wins. Every time.

QUESTIONS TO PONDER

1. Of the four aspects of emotional connection, which are you better at?

2. When is the best time for you and your tween to emotionally connect?

3. How would you describe your biggest challenge to connect with your tween?

4. If you are divorced or do not live with your tween's other parent, what is one thing you can do to promote your tween's relationship with that parent?

PART TWO

It's Not You,
It's Neuroscience

The Tween Brain

"You could call it brain sculpting, or brain nourishing, or brain building.
Whatever phrase you prefer, the point is crucial and thrilling:
As a result of the words we use and the actions we take, children's brains
will actually change, be built, as they undergo new experiences."

—DANIEL J. SIEGEL, MD, PSYCHIATRIST,
EXECUTIVE DIRECTOR OF MINDSET INSTITUTE

"Start children off on the way they should go,
and even when they are old they will not turn from it."

—PROVERBS 22:6 NIV

Our children are blessings in our lives—each with their own gifts and unique characteristics. We know this, and there is plenty in our faith teachings to reinforce it. However, as with most everything in our lives, even the good stuff, it's never all fun and games. With our tween, sometimes we really get them. At other times, we do not. We are left asking, *Who Are You & What Have You Done with My Kid?*...They are not like us or they are different from what we thought they would be. We want to see their purpose and help them find their path, but it's not always clear. The haze can work our last nerve or drive us to despair. Fortunately, there is much support in our faith teachings, a powerful wind at our back, to strengthen our ability to persevere as we work to make constructive parenting choices and overcome the hurdles we encounter. Our faith also tells us, the best help comes when we help ourselves, and that often starts with knowledge. In parenting our tween, that means understanding where they are neurologically. This is the gateway to grasping why they behave the way they do and finding the patience to parent in ways that build emotional connection.

It isn't easy being a tween. As they transition from elementary school to middle school, the pressure piles on: Academic expectations ramp up, social media inundates them, and their friendships change—sometimes with devastating effect. Meanwhile, *they're* changing. Fast. Overnight, they go from acting and thinking like a child to making more complex social and emotional connections. They're referencing information and using phrases they didn't learn at home. (My sixth grader came home from school with the phrase "word choice" not too long ago. Seriously!)

And because these changes happen so quickly, tweens can feel uncertain and insecure in their thoughts and ideas. Often they do not know how to maneuver with any semblance of grace, especially boys. (That hyper, obnoxious, impulsive behavior you may be seeing in your boy? It's perfectly natural, as much as it may be driving you nuts.) Girls typically reach the psychological and emotional changes earlier than boys, which is why tween girls often behave more maturely and responsibly, particularly in the classroom, though it can also lead to the mean girl messes that surface in middle school (more on this later in the chapter).

As confusing as this can be for parents, there are perfectly logical, science-based reasons for all this craziness, and we can use them to shape our tween's brain, their habits, and our relationship with them in the way we parent. Those science-based reasons amount to these four truths:

- Tween brains are changing.
- Tweens experience emotions they do not recognize.
- Tweens are socially awkward.
- Above all, tweens do not know how to express themselves.

What follows is a deeper look at each of these.

CHAPTER FOUR

TWEEN BRAINS ARE CHANGING

Quite simply, tweens aren't equipped neurologically to react the way we expect, wish, or hope they would. That's because the tween years are a time of profound neurobiological change and development. Remember in Part One: Love Wins how we compared the nervous system to an operating system of a computer, unseen but powering all activity? Now think of *your tween's brain as that computer* in the midst of a software update. Once the "download" is complete (which can take until they're in their mid-twenties!), they will be able to process experiences quickly, think through decisions safely, and control their emotions more effectively.

Until then, we're going to see bad choices, a shortage of wisdom, awkward social behaviors, and a lack of emotional control. Our kids are like Spider-Man after he was first bitten and realized he could shoot webs from his wrist. At first he was shooting them all over the room and getting frustrated because he couldn't make sense of what he could do. He had all this amazing *ability* but couldn't *use* it. Eventually he got the hang of it: He found his confidence and learned how to aim those webs. His superpower was born. In a similar way, our tween's brain is developing and growing. They are making their way to their superpowers, but it takes time.

Over the past twenty-five years, neuroscientists have discovered a great deal about the architecture and function of the brain, including just how developmentally important the very small four-year window of "tweenhood" is in a child's life. It's not just those first five years that matter so much. It *all* counts, especially the tween years. Previously, neuroscientists attributed the reckless, impulsive, disrespectful, and emotional behavior seen in tweens to "raging hormones." When they honed in on the pre-adolescent-to-adolescent (aka tween!) brain, scientists were astounded to find massive brain growth in the neural circuitry. Translation: As the tween brain takes in new information, it is literally growing like a vine, an explosion of neural connections like new leaves…and the growth is wild, producing a labyrinth of thoughts and feelings the tween has never had before.

These are the culprits behind tween behavior, and all of it is happening *before* the onset of hormonal puberty. It peaks at about age eleven for girls and twelve for boys, and it's completely changing how we look at the way tweens conduct themselves.

With this growing mountain of information about brain changes and how they relate developmentally to our kids—impacting their emotions, behaviors, and relationships—we can start to connect what is happening in our tween's brain to the strategies needed to shape it. We can use this knowledge to create peace in our home, to build that all-important emotional connection, and to set the stage for the best life possible for our tween and ourselves! For parents, it's a gold mine. What we learn here will help us understand our tween and get the most from the parenting tools and techniques I cover later in the book.

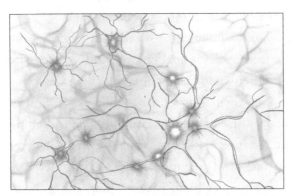

The tween brain: nerve cells taking in information and growing explosively

First Vines

It starts during pregnancy. In the months before birth, the brain produces its first burst of neural connections—that initial vine of intertwining information. It is our body's way of preparing our unborn child to engage in the world they are about to enter. In fact, when they are born, our babies have more neural connections than adults do!

The next growth spurt happens when our child is between two and five years old. This is when they advance from the reflexive, reactive behaviors of babies to get what they need (think hungry/wet/tired…cry) to processing and storing information. They start to understand cause and effect. They're learning about free will, sorting their lives into things they like (comfort) and things they don't (discomfort), and behaving accordingly. They deploy a more sophisticated mix of verbal and nonverbal communication to get not just what they *need*, but what they *want*. They use their words, they stomp their feet, they cross their arms, they run away. This is why toddlers start to boycott veggies, bedtime, and rules, and beg to read books with parents, eat candy, and play outside. Then they store what they learn, which leads to repeat behaviors.

I see it all day long with my five-year-old, Livvy: Going for a walk the other day was not fun. It was cold outside, uncomfortable. Watching *Blippi* on the computer was fun, like putting on big, comfy slippers. Now she knows: *Blippi* equals awesome! Going for a walk? Not awesome. Welcome to pushback. Plainly, we are drawn to the things that give us pleasure or comfort at every age: The trick is to make sure these things are life-giving rather than life-limiting. In Livvy's case, it's up to us, her parents, to help her manage this, which brings me to our tween.

In the Garden of Tween

The explosion of neural growth during the tween years is mind-blowing—figuratively and literally—and it shakes our tween to their core. Each new connection between neurons adds yet another piece of information they will use to observe, assess, and behave in their world. Multiply that by thousands, millions, and more, and you start to get the picture of just how dense this intertwining vine of new thoughts, ideas, and information grows to be. Our tween is like a sponge, taking in everything around them and processing, processing, processing. They enter their tween years as a very kidlike nine-year-old with zero control over or insight into their emotions and very little ability to communicate thoughts and feelings. They progress to a twelve-year-old who starts to exhibit the more adultlike behaviors we discussed in Part One and put words to emotions as they try new behaviors and communication strategies such as:

- Asking questions to gain more insight
- Pointing out our contradictions to trip us up in our thinking
- Negotiating for what they want
- Defying the rules
- Lying
- Explaining their position with more clarity and conviction
- Offering a friendly compromise or amendment

The black-and-white "I like it"/"I don't like it" of their younger years is more nuanced, complex. They're linking ideas, thoughts, and concepts and beginning to develop abstract reasoning. It's why we see more independence, personal choice, and new behaviors that originate outside the family. The person inside our tween is starting to take shape through the words they use, their thoughts and behavior and—most interesting— the *meaning* they apply to their thoughts and behavior. In other words, they are developing strong opinions about what they think of others, how they view world issues, and what they think of us as parents! Their opinions are starting to be based on things happening around them, and they are checking in with us parents to see what we think.

However, with the overload of new neural connections jamming the pathways of their brain and the lack of experience needed to help them understand all they're feeling, our tween is like a weathervane when the wind is coming from all directions, spinning and unsure where to aim their thoughts. In the midst of all this, with their newfound ability to link ideas together and focus on meaning (even when they misread a situation), they are trying out different behaviors, working through steps, particularly as they relate to their peers: for example, *If I wear this, how does everyone act toward me?* or *If I do X, will people like me?* There's meaning tied to *everything* and many shades of all emotion. It's not just pain or pleasure. It's joy or sadness, acceptance or denial, feeling good about themselves or not…all this nuance in the middle of that dense vine!

And it happens suddenly. It's like one day they wake up and the world looks completely different. And just as a vine crawls throughout the garden, penetrating every corner, these neural connections travel across all regions of the brain.

Eventually the brain will send messages between its different regions to think quickly, make good choices, manage emotion, and live productively. Remember that download? What's critical during the tween years is the groundwork that is being laid for the habits and patterns of behavior to come.

In our developing tween, the parts of the brain we are most concerned with are the frontal lobe and the limbic system, which is in the temporal lobe, toward the back of the brain. The frontal lobe is home of the prefrontal cortex, seat of critical thinking and comprehension. It controls impulses and decision making. The frontal lobe is also responsible for personality, concentration, planning, problem solving, speech, smell, movement, and emotional reactions. Self-awareness lives here as well.

Tween Traits

- Egocentric
- Literal-minded
- Live in the present
- Linear thinkers
- Visually oriented
- Look to heroes
- Starting to be individuals

The temporal lobe is where we process what we see and hear, and how we use language. It's where we create and preserve memories through the hippocampus, which is in the limbic system. The limbic system monitors reflexive emotions such as fear and anxiety through the amygdala, the emotional center of our brain and the source of our fight-or-flight impulse. When the amygdala floods, our prefrontal cortex leaves the building.

Brain Anatomy

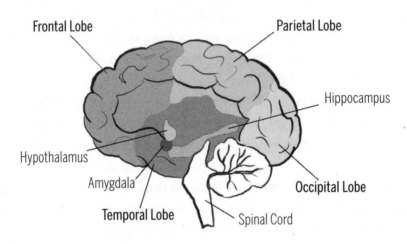

How Habits Form

So our tween has all these new neural connections weighing in on the way they think and behave. Imagine being in a crowded room where everybody is talking at once. What do you hear? What claims your attention? At some point, the loudest voices win. That's how the brain operates as well: It literally prunes away seldom-used thoughts and behaviors (aka neural connections) that is, the "quiet" voices, and keeps the "loudest." By trimming away unused (unheard) or rarely accessed (quiet) neural connections, the brain becomes more efficient and quicker at accessing information that is needed on a more regular basis. Picture a jam-packed garage. You toss the rusting jogger you haven't used since your tween was a toddler so that you can more easily get to the bike you ride every chance you get. Pruning is like that, and it happens in late adolescence.

This is how habits form, but the stage is set during the tween years for the pruning to come. These are the practice rounds. The more our tween behaves in a particular way, choosing one activity over another, the easier it is for them to repeat the behavior, which creates a well-traveled pathway in the brain: Something feels good, the reward circuit ignites, and our tween wants more of it. They've got a million things they can do with all these sprouting neural connections, and whichever ones they repeat over and over are going to be kept and the rest are going to be chopped away, pruned. Bye-bye excess vines.

In reality, it looks something like this: A tween plays video games, gets excited and wants to play *more* video games. Either they will play more *or* parents will set boundaries, teaching the tween the benefits of delayed gratification. The brain will code the experience in one of two ways: 1) It registers the excitement our tween feels, building an *I-want-more-video-games, I-want-more-video-games, I-want-more-video-games* impulse (despite the mental numbing that grows along with it). Or 2) they will learn to tolerate the discomfort of discipline, redirection, and delayed gratification through us, their parents. Brain shaping is how I like to describe it. The upside of this is, over time, our tween will feel good about good choices and gravitate to them.

Will they fight us? Sure. That's normal. We want them to have that fight. It will serve them well in life, and we need to allow space for it. It's one of the ways they practice their voice, go after something they want, make a name for themselves. One day, the fight will go to good use: when they apply to college, hone their talents, apply for a job requiring a little more experience than they have.

Over time, the brain will strengthen the path to the behavior repeated most often, making it easier and easier to do. Consider that our tween may make the same choice twenty times a day for years and you can start to see how practice can make perfect...or imperfect. (Accustom the brain to equating reward with the nonsense of never-ending video games, and nonsense is where it will go, because it hasn't experienced discipline or any other alternative.)

Not only that, the brain will apply the pattern of thinking that is most familiar to other experiences of immediate or delayed gratification—friends, drinking, etc. It's like this: So now our tween is in college. They have an exam. Their friends are going out. Will they stay in to study or blow it off for whatever their friends are doing? Their choice will hinge on what they learned when they were younger, especially during their tween years with all the brain activity they experienced. Did they learn delayed gratification and how to follow through, or did they learn to quit?

The Root of Addiction

An odd thing happens with unproductive repeat behaviors such as binge watching, gaming, eating junk food, and more: They become mind-numbing, leaving us feeling underwhelmed, tired, and even bored, yet wanting more. The brain returns again and again to what it has been trained to think of as a source of excitement, pleasure, and/or comfort. We know as adults there's no way that third drink feels as good as the first. In a similar way, tweens and teens have both told me that at some point playing video games or watching "another episode on Netflix" is no longer fun. "I'm just doing it," they say, further imbedding a craving for instant gratification. It puts the brain at risk for addictive behavior (including substance abuse), and it can start (or be stopped) during the tween years. A genetic predisposition to addiction can compound the problem; some brains are more apt to latch on to addictive behaviors than others. It's in the DNA. That's why we often see substance abuse issues run through a family tree...all the more reason to teach our tween to make life-giving choices.

As parents, naturally, we want to make sure the brain is practicing the good habits that lead to self-confidence, resilience, and connection. If our tween feels emotionally close to us, safe in their interactions with us and in the delayed-gratification boundaries we set, guess what neural connections will *not* be pruned? As we learned in Part One, when we are emotionally connected with our tween, their brain is calm, they feel good. They create cell memory around this. With repeat experience, the memories are reinforced, and our tween will behave in ways that bring them more of this great, calm feeling. They won't even know they're doing it.

As I said earlier, our tween may not appreciate all of our efforts to instill good habits. In fact, they will rage against us, rest assured. Still, as they get older, they will remember the comfort of their close relationship with us and look to replicate it in their relationships outside the family more than they will remember their pushback.

In the same way, tweens who practice the tenacity and follow-through required to succeed academically and in extracurriculars such as music, sports, or any number of other interests will hardwire these connections, and they will seek the rewards they have always found in creative thinking, physical activity, learning, and any of the other activities they pursue in their younger years.

The Long Haul—Why It Matters

Once all these habits and patterns of behavior—neural connections—that originated and were practiced during the tween years travel with our child through their teenage years and survive the pruning process, the brain locks them in place by coating nerve cell axons with a white sealant-type substance. Axons are the long, thin tendrils extending from nerve cells that connect them to one another and transmit information throughout the brain, strengthening and accelerating communication between cells and through different brain regions. It's a process called myelination, a kind of "save as" for a "document" that was begun in middle school. During the tween years, the "document" was a draft, easily edited. (You know the saying about old dogs and new tricks? This is where it comes from. When brains are young, it's easier to create habits and break them. Our brains are more malleable. It's called neuroplasticity.)

Myelination is what gives the twenty-something-year-old the ability to think faster, make better choices, remember previous experiences, improve performance, and control their emotions. It is an exciting and transformative neurobiological phenomenon that imprints on the emotions, thoughts, and behaviors of the adult our tween will become. But it can also lock in life-limiting habits and behaviors. It's why it's so important particularly to protect children from trauma and what we therapists call "attachment injuries." This is the damage done when their closest relationships are broken…by parenting or family relationships that are volatile, overly critical, judgmental, inconsistent, or absent, unsafe, frightening, and unreliable, for whatever reason. (You will read more about this in Part Three: What Lies Beneath.)

Because here's the thing: It's not easy, but we can change ingrained behaviors, despite the pruning and myelination that have set them in place. A student can develop study habits in college; it's possible to cultivate new discipline. The brain has the plasticity for this. However, emotional injuries from relationship train wrecks are *really* hard to reverse. The brain does not want to let go of behaviors caused by these, even to the point of destroying future relationships. Still, it's never hopeless, just hard.

CHAPTER FIVE

TWEENS EXPERIENCE EMOTIONS THEY DO NOT RECOGNIZE

While the vine of neuronal connections is twisting through our tween's brain, the way they experience and express emotions changes drastically. They feel things brand-new to them, and those feelings can be very powerful. Yet tweens don't yet have the experience or any of the maturity needed to recognize what they're feeling, so they cannot put words to it. They don't understand why they feel so emotional. Simultaneously, they have very limited ability to control their emotions, which can put them in a kind of I'm-the-only-one-going-through-this space. All this is unsettling to a tween, compounding the insecurity they already feel from so much change. This winds up making our tween even more emotional. So we may notice a new moodiness in our tween or hyper-sensitivity to their emotions and those of others. They anger easily and irrationally, over things that seem minor. This is also why they may sometimes seem withdrawn.

The emotional temperament of a tween starts to show up more in their day-to-day experiences. Here's why: Neuronal sprouting and pruning starts in the back of the brain—the limbic system—and ends in the prefrontal cortex. Remember, as we covered earlier, the limbic system is the part of the brain (that is, the nervous system) that connects emotional responses to experiences and sensory information. It is where emotion is *processed* and memories are consolidated. As you'll also recall, the prefrontal cortex is the part of the brain that controls impulses, thinks critically, makes decisions, solves problems, plans, and weighs consequences. It is where acting responsibly comes from. It is also the last to go through myelination. So this part of the brain that will one day provide the calm rationality and perspective we need to balance us when we are overexcited, upset, afraid, frustrated, or insecure is not yet able to help our tween.

What's more, the limbic system, our tween's primary source of feedback for how to behave, is growing and changing. So, while the limbic system—our tween's emotional center—is growing, the prefrontal cortex—our tween's thinking center—is sleeping, unavailable for consultation.

So, when a parent says, "Brush your teeth," a teacher says, "Listen," or a friend says, "You're really good at something," these experiences evoke newly intense feelings such as joy, rage, fear, excitement, or insecurity. The emotional response is quick, without much thought, and extreme. (Remember, the prefrontal cortex is offline.) This is why tween behavior can feel out of left field, tantrumlike, confusing, or offensive.

In real terms it can look like this: Our tween pops off when we ask them—*for the fourth time*—to clean their room. By late adolescence, they will be able to pause and think for a second before they react to the request. Hopefully, we parents have trained their brain to involve the prefrontal cortex to say, *Sure, why not, it feels good to be in a clean room anyway.* But don't look for that in the tween years. They don't yet have the neural connections for it.

CHAPTER SIX

TWEENS ARE SOCIALLY AWKWARD

Is there anyone who longs to repeat middle school? For most of us, it was not our finest hour of feeling confident, happy, and well-adjusted. And that makes sense: With all the brain changes, the tween years are often loaded with angst, embarrassment, and insecurity. It is the lowest point of self-esteem and the peak of bullying and mean girl behavior.

Mean Girls in Middle School:
They May Not Be What You Think

The bullying stereotypical of middle school girls (and boys to some extent) is much more about chasing a shiny peer prize or expressing control where they can than intentional cruelty. And it makes sense, right? Tweens don't have the brain development or emotional experience to think up and execute a sophisticated or premeditated plan to hurtfully bully their peers. Mean girls and bullies typically don't know they are hurting others, nor do they mean to.

As toddlers, kids play side by side with little overlap or engagement with one another. In elementary school, kids move on to playing together. Supervised by parents and teachers, they learn to create rules and cooperate with one another. By the tween years, play is peer led.

It's a tween's first go at being a friend, independent of adults and their reminders to "Be nice," "Share your toys," or "Say thank you." Meanwhile, tweens are trying to figure out the social structure and how to cope with their own big emotions.

It's like they see a window up high, and they are trying to reach it to see what's on the other side. Maybe they are suffering with family problems or school problems, so they want to see in the "window of relief." Or perhaps they see a popular group and they want to see in the "window of being cool." In the process of getting to the window, they may reject or say painful, scarring things to others, even long-term friends. Tweens will also push away from kids that make them look or feel bad by comparison. They don't really understand that they're pushing to get rid of the thing that doesn't feel good. Remember how self-focused tweens are. It is all about them. Empathy is still under development.

They may also bully as an outlet for the dysfunction that is beyond their control in other areas of their life. A sort of *I feel bad. I can't call my dad out on his behavior. My mom's never going to be on my side. My teachers don't understand me. I don't even know what I'd say if I could, because nobody's taught me so I dump on that weak kid over there.* Again, these are feelings and behaviors tweens aren't equipped neurologically to even begin to understand.

Friendships often change, becoming less reliable, as development creates a gap in interests and abilities. For instance, some tweens are still playing with dolls or coloring while others have moved on to music, fashion trends, and crushes. Some have matured physically while others have not. There can also be an eighteen-month age spread in one grade, which can make for an even greater developmental divide. In addition, most school districts merge several elementary schools into one middle school, which exposes our tween to different peer groups and fair-weather friendships. This new uncertainty in friendship can create a life-or-death experience for tweens that leads to peer pressure, super-charged emotionality around friendship, and a preoccupation with how they fit into their social group.

To tweens, friends and how they are seen by others are matters of survival, and given their predisposition to respond extremely to just about everything, it's no wonder! To be a tween without a peer group can feel like being alone in the wild without food, water, or anything to hunt with. A tween without friends feels vulnerable, rejected, insecure, *and* under a microscope, as if everyone is aware of their situation. In contrast, to have friends makes a tween know they matter to someone else in a world that is important to them.

We may hear our tween talk about their group of friends or a sports team they are part of or another tween they are interested in. Social interactions take a more prominent role in their daily lives, yet they don't know what's hitting them. It's their first go with all this. They are more about having friends and being around peers than looking for meaningful friendship. (That comes in the teen years.) Tweens just want to be accepted by their peers and feel like they are part of the crowd. When they are not, they devise all kinds of reasons why it might be happening, they worry about it, and then they worry some more.

Meanwhile, friendship and our tween's desire to be liked is comingled with the newfound awareness of self, independence, and identity as a person outside the family that we talked about earlier. They start asking questions such as: "Who am I?" "How do I fit in the world around me?" "Do people like me?" "Where am I good?" "Where am I bad?" They are trying to figure out their worth both in their family and in their peer group.

They will likely try different clothing styles, ways of speaking and of presenting themselves to see how different personas feel and how their peer group responds. For instance, one week they may want to dress like a rapper, then the next like an athlete. They might talk in a funny slang one week then return to their old dialect the next. They may try to be a comic, a leader, a follower, a rebel. It's like a new form of dress-up. This is also why when we ask a tween for their opinion, they tend to be noncommittal, responding with "I guess" or "It's okay." They don't know if what they say is going to land well with their peers, and they want to be able to change their mind.

Happy in the Library

With all the focus on peers and "fitting in," why are some tweens so happy in the library, on the periphery of the social scene? It can confound parents. Not to worry. Some tweens are simply more introverted. They find their rewards in good grades, spending time alone, creating things by themselves. They may also have support in other areas of their life—from sports, family, or a skill such as music—that is grounding them and building their self-confidence. If your tween is an introvert, recognize the gift for what it is. If they are pursuing healthy activities (rather than unlimited video gaming for example), we must resist the urge to push them to be more social. The last thing we want to do is pressure them to feel like they "should be around other kids more" when they feel good reading and doing homework. Instead, we can make sure they don't feel alone and they are involved in activities that bring them joy and contentment. They *will* learn to socialize. They will not miss out on that. It just might look different from what you think.

They are utterly focused on themselves and how they measure up in the world, so they think others must notice them too. In fact, tweens feel as if everyone is looking at them, seeing what they are doing, evaluating and talking about them. This is why we might see our tween looking at the school yearbook for hours, identifying the best athletes, who is academically superior or popular, what video games their peers play, how others look, and what they are wearing. They are preparing for the daily battle of fitting in and measuring up, wondering:

"How do I compare to my friend or the most popular kid?"
"What makes him the most popular kid or good at math?"
"What does she or he think of me?"
"Do I look cool?"
"Do I act cool?"

This hyper-awareness of themselves and their peers takes up a significant part of our tween's emotional energy. While tweens do not yet have the language to describe what is happening internally, they do feel everyone can tell they are freaking out inside. The pressure is intense and real. Consider the middle school dance…kids hanging on the sidelines, talking and teasing one another. Perhaps some will dance, but rarely is there an I-like-you, you-like-me interaction. On the contrary, if our tween likes someone, they probably won't talk to them. If there's any interaction at all, it will be the friend of the friend who likes the tween acting on their behalf. You can cut the anxiety in the room with a knife.

Complicating things further, there is enough improvement in our tween's abstract reasoning to be dangerous: They can wonder what peers are thinking of them and believe they are detecting whether or not they are liked. In reality, they lack the ability to see multiple perspectives, think through potential options, and solve problems. Add in their impulsivity (remember, the prefrontal cortex is not around at this point in our child's life to help them take a more measured, rational approach, which leaves their emotional limbic system home alone and in charge), and we have a tween who sees their peers looking at them and jumps to conclusions thinking they are not smart enough, wearing the right clothes, or good at athletics. (The egocentric mind of a tween imagines their peers are thinking only about them. The irony is, most likely, their peers are thinking only about themselves!)

If our tween is well-liked, they feel it in their nervous system: Their body is calm, they have less anxiety or fear. In contrast, if our tween is bullied, teased, left out, or last to be chosen, we are more apt to see symptoms of depression such as trouble sleeping or emotional eating. Or we may see them becoming easily irritated, isolating themselves, avoiding certain activities, and experience racing thoughts—all symptoms of anxiety.

Now factor in how the tween brain will recognize behavioral patterns that get a desired result and repeat them—over and over. For example, when they dress a certain way and their peers respond positively, our tween will dress like that again. This is where peer pressure is so powerful. In addition, the brain also recognizes behaviors that are not getting a desired result, and a tween will veer away from them. Sometimes we see a tween who does well in school stop taking school work seriously after getting picked on, choosing instead to focus on peer relationships and being seen as cool to avoid being left alone, rejected, or misunderstood.

Experiences of feeling safe, close, and comforted—like someone responded to us—or, conversely, experiences of feeling threatened or isolated contribute to our attachment style, that is, how we form relationships with others. As our child approaches their tween years, what they know about attachment is from infancy and childhood. In their tween years, their attachment style is influenced by friendship as well, trauma too, but we'll get to all this in Part Three: What Lies Beneath. I bring it up here because it is stunning to me how many adults I work with talk about the impact on their lives of middle school peer relationships (including bullies and mean girls): The brain remembers, intuitively, and that has long-term ramifications for our kids as well.

Our Tween at Home

Despite all this new focus on friends, *mom and dad still matter*. In fact, we are essential during the tween years. Tweens aren't ready to count solely on their peers for their relational needs. They want to make sure they are getting this peer thing right, so they will look to us for support until they get the hang of it later during adolescence. So don't underestimate how much they need us and look to us for guidance, even if it doesn't seem like it. When we are able to vibe with our tween, we are able to pick up on their emotional cues, soothe them, and create a secure base from which they can launch into the world of friends, challenges, hard decisions, new experiences, and decision making. They need a source of strength and resiliency that will be their guiding light through the difficult waters they are starting to experience. They need us!

CHAPTER SEVEN

TWEENS DO NOT KNOW
HOW TO EXPRESS THEMSELVES

Tweens are not yet equipped with the critical thinking ability needed to understand and communicate the social and emotional changes they are experiencing and how they are being affected. They lack the language to explain things they think and feel, so they can seem awkward and act strangely. This too is perfectly in line with where tweens are neurologically.

When *teens* come into my office, they want their parents to leave. When *tweens* come in for initial sessions, they want their parents present. However, tweens will share very little in front of their parents because they are embarrassed and unsure what to say. They still want guidance from their parents; they will even let them do the talking. It's almost as if they are afraid of being too independent or making a mistake, so they permit their parents to steer the conversation.

When parents do leave the room, I've discovered tweens have a lot on their minds and will share but often don't have the words to articulate their thoughts. Coupled with the embarrassment and concern about getting it wrong (that worry stays in the room even when their parents depart), I often see tweens are self-conscious talking about what's on their minds as well as insecure because of the uncharted territory in which they find themselves. They have never felt these feelings or experienced all of these social dilemmas. However, once tweens open up and relax, they tend to feel better. There is relief in being heard and understood, knowing that what they are experiencing is not unusual. It reassures them that they are okay.

Tangled Vines: About Mental Illness

The rapid growth of the tween brain can also surface a predisposition to mental illness. In fact, about 70 percent of mental illnesses, including anxiety, mood and eating disorders, and psychosis, start to appear during this stage of brain development. As connections are pruned away and others become more prominent in later adolescence, a predisposed mental health issue can become pronounced.

Mental health issues are carried in the brain and passed down from one generation to the next. Like substance abuse, they show up throughout a family tree. Sometimes they are exacerbated by unproductive behaviors practiced during the tween years…things such as skipping school, quitting activities, emotional eating, sleeping odd hours, negative thought patterns, loathing self-talk, self-doubt, or getting lost in television.

The key is to catch mental illness or addictive behavior as early as possible and identify the resources that will provide the best support and coping systems for both tween and parent.

Early signs of mental illness and/or addictive behavior include:

- **Change in Mood**
  Particularly if the mood remains unchanged through a range of experiences—good, tough, or neutral. For example, an outgoing tween who was always around becomes quiet and retreats more often to their room; a tween who is usually quiet and calm becomes whiny, clingy, easily frustrated, or emotionally explosive. It can be hard to tease out the normal mood changes of tween development shifts from something more serious. But when there is a combination of changes, it is worth a deeper look.

- **Negative Self-talk**
  This is a common early sign that a tween is struggling. It is one thing for a tween to say, "I am so dumb" after receiving a bad grade. It is another if they are calling themselves "dumb," "ugly," or saying things such as "No one likes me" or "It's never going to get better" for no discernible reason, particularly if they don't seem able to shake the negative self-talk.

- **Lower Energy Than Usual**
  If a tween has less energy than usual, we must consider the source and duration of these bouts. "Tired over the weekend" is no cause for concern. Tired throughout the day on most days for a week or longer is.

- **Behavioral Changes**
  This can include anything from dropping out of activities they used to like, eating more when they aren't hungry, or picking at their food and not eating (both signs of emotional eating), and leaving friends who they can grow and learn from in favor of new friendships with tweens who are struggling, to playing endless hours of video games, spending an inordinate amount of time on their phone, or simply doing nothing.

If you see milder signs of any of the above in your tween, start by asking questions in a gentle, caring, curious way. (We'll talk more about how to do this in later chapters when we cover *seeing* and *hearing* our tween.) Find out if they will share their feelings, worries, things that are bothering them, emotions they feel they can't get past. Also see if you can brainstorm together ways to cope with their struggles, ways to use their voice to be assertive, and discuss when you as a parent should step in.

If your concerns persist or your tween is not open to discussing the shifts you are noticing, you will want to reach out to the school, coaches, or other adults in your tween's life to determine if they are witnessing similar behaviors. This helps a parent determine if the changes are developmental or attributable to exhaustion and a desire to just let their hair down at home. Tweens usually can't hide a mental health issue, so if there is one, others will have noticed it as well.

If you are seeing extreme behavior changes or suspect eating and bingeing, cutting, stealing or other illegal activities, substance use (alcohol, marijuana, pills), or, obviously, if your tween is sharing suicidal thoughts, start with a good assessment to determine if there is an immediate need for medical attention, an inpatient program, or safety watch.

For concerns just beginning to appear, talk with your tween's school about educational accommodations, speak to your child's pediatrician or a leader of your faith community, or seek individual or family therapy.

We the Brain Changers

Tweens are at the beginning of a new life adventure. The brain is preparing for all the people, places, and things they will know. It's a perfect time for us to connect with our tween…to be a source of understanding, caring, and joy. They will put these experiences in their pocket and take them through adolescence and adulthood, into relationships, and it will positively affect how they feel about themselves.

Parents, mentors, teachers, and other supportive adults become *brain changers* able to mold the tween brain with repeated exposure to life experiences that activate positive behaviors, patterns, and emotional expression. The more exposure tweens get to this "good stuff" such as goal-directed behavior, the more likely the brain will naturally gravitate to it and the better our tween will be able to manage their actions and emotions as they get older. In the same spirit, the less used "bad stuff" will be pruned away. In other words, we want to encourage the brain to keep what will be helpful and useful throughout life and purge what will not. The primal wisdom of the Bible tells us the same. As you may recall from the beginning of this part: "Start children off on the way they should go, and even when they are old, they will not turn from it." This is from Proverbs 22:6, and it's powerful.

You'll learn more about brain shaping in the chapters to come, particularly in Section Two: Your Toolbox. However, to use the tools I present there most effectively, we need to understand—drumroll, please—ourselves and the role we play in shaping our own patterns of communication and our relationships. That's up next!

QUESTIONS TO PONDER

1. What childlike behaviors do you see in your tween? What adultlike behaviors do you see?

2. As you interact with your tween and observe them in social and family situations, can you see their focus on self, which is so prevalent at this developmental stage? Can you see how literal they are? How they live in the present?

3. What behaviors do you see in your tween that appear to be turning into habits, and what role might your parenting be playing in the habits you see forming?

4. Would you say your tween is a social butterfly or content to spend more time by themselves than you would like?

PART THREE

What Lies Beneath

Let's Dig Deeper

"By exploring the inner-workings of the parental brain,
they reveal what happens neurochemically when caregiving skills
are strong—leading to healthy attachment—and when they
are impaired, or 'blocked,' potentially leading to a host
of behavioral and emotional problems in kids."

—DANIEL HUGHES, CLINICAL PSYCHOLOGIST AND FOUNDER
OF DYADIC DEVELOPMENTAL PSYCHOTHERAPY

"Not only so, but we also glory in our sufferings,
because we know that suffering produces perseverance;
perseverance, character; and character, hope."

—ROMANS 5:1–5 NIV

Calling all parents. Yes, you, me, all of us: While no one is more important to us than our children, and we *want* to do our best for them, driven by primal impulses rooted in our brain, it doesn't always turn out that way. The journey of humanity inevitably takes us off course from God's plan, and sometimes our best intentions veer off a cliff, leaving us stranded from each other, often surprising us in a *How did* that *happen?!* kind of way. Perhaps someone has treated us poorly and we are having trouble bouncing back, or maybe we are stuck in a lifestyle that leaves us with little time and patience for parenting.

To get back to our tween, we must remember, first and foremost, we are only human, with the same needs as our tween to be loved, comforted, and forgiven, and there are reasons why things derail…reasons we can identify and address. It just requires some digging.

It's like this: You move into a house; perhaps you've even built it yourself. It sits on a piece of land. The view is great. What a future you see! The thing is, we sometimes get so caught up in the view we forget to look at the ground beneath us—the *soil* on which our house sits. Perhaps there are contamination or water issues, or rocky bedrock causing uneven ground. If so, our house will have problems. So we have three choices: ignore the problems and hope for the best (denial), move (denial, denial), or remediate the soil to create a solid base and a way forward.

In the same way, our past is *our* soil—complete with the good earth (there's *always* some of that) and any unaddressed bedrock, water, or contamination issues. As we get older and new experiences pile on—the daily demands of our lives, the challenges, traumas, and triumphs—our soil shifts. For better or worse, it is the foundation from which we parent and build our own families. It determines how we mold our tween to respond to and process *their* life experiences and relationships. Not only do we "raise our tween," we establish *their* soil, present always in their memory and nervous system no matter how old they get, just as it is for us. **You see, our history doesn't stay in the past; it may lay dormant and seem unimportant—for years.** *Until we have families of our own.* **And then the soil on which we are building our family is revealed—in our feelings and behaviors toward our partner and our kids.**

CHAPTER EIGHT

LEARNING FROM OUR PAST

As we move into the self-examination to come in this chapter and in Part Four: Remediating Our Soil, it is important to take a breath and remember the reassurance we find in our faith teachings—there is a plan for each one of us filled with comfort, security, and joy. And suffering. And out of suffering we will learn and grow, feel contentment and peace. We will be stronger, and we will be models of support and strength for others. We won't always see how this all fits together, and often it will feel unfair, but it does make sense and will lead us to where we need to be—thanks be to God— something bigger than us, however you make sense of it.

Anguish is our call to shed something in us that is toxic or broken. With the grace and wisdom we find in our faith, we are able to view ourselves with honest clarity, process any pain we may be holding on to, and understand that the challenges given to us in life help us develop endurance, strength of character, hope, and ultimately joy. We can use what we learn to change ourselves and any legacy we may have been handed. We can also use it to help our children through their challenges—in the actions and insights we share from what we've learned.

As we take what can be hard steps and learn from any pain we may have experienced in our past, we must also remember we are not alone in the journey to the other side of it: Whether we believe in God or not, He believes in us and holds us when we are hurting, especially in our darkest moments. It is from all this love and positive energy coming our way that we find courage to look where perhaps we'd rather not. It's critical that we do, because the better we know ourselves—where we are strong or where we are likely to get stuck as a parent...

- The more able we will be to heal the past hurts and fears that may be throwing up roadblocks between us and our kids.
- The greater the chance that we will not pass down to our kids the wounds and anxieties we have carried with us from our past.
- The better we will be at recognizing and channeling our strengths to parent our tweens in a way that nurtures and builds emotional connection.
- The stronger we will be as men and women living the lifestyle that is authentic to our deeper self.

To pull this off, first we need to understand a bit about our caregiver system. We all have one.

The Caregiver System

When we become parents, self-centered morphs to child-centered thanks to a specific set of hormones and brain functions in charge of parent–child bonding. Together, they make up our caregiver system. Our ability to love our children is based on this system. Here's how it works (or doesn't).

Our Helping Hormones

- **Oxytocin:** It's also called "the bonding hormone" and is often more pronounced in women. Oxytocin triggers nurturing and prompts us to find interactions with our children enjoyable. We release it when we hold our infant, hug, exchange smiles, and participate in other bonding acts. The more responsive and loving we are, the more oxytocin we release. Oxytocin receptors are located in the limbic system's amygdala—no surprise there, given the amygdala's role as the emotional center of our brain, as you will recall from Part Two: It's Not You, It's Neuroscience. It's no surprise either that with oxytocin on the scene, we are calm, the amygdala's fight-or-flight-response is caged and silent. *Without* oxytocin, we are defensive and withdrawn. What's particularly interesting is that it is possible to ignite an oxytocin release, to reverse the negative path its absence creates, with intentional choices to hug, smile, bond.

- **Dopamine:** This is "the happy hormone." We release it when we feel pleasure, such as when we are enjoying time with our children. It activates our reward system. We feel warmth and joy. Dopamine triggers are stored in our memory so that even anticipation of a triggering event (for example, time with our kids), will initiate a dopamine release. While it's a natural, unconscious process, we *can* actually teach our brain to release dopamine by intentionally creating happy experiences with our kids, just as we can train ourselves to release oxytocin.

A parent whose brain releases oxytocin and dopamine will parent differently than one who doesn't get that jolt. We will talk more about how to generate oxytocin and dopamine and use them to emotionally connect with our children and improve our parenting in Part Four: Remediating Our Soil.

CHAPTER NINE

THE BRAIN CONNECTION

The brain functions in our caregiver system consist of messages sent between our prefrontal cortex (center of our critical thinking, emotional regulation, and executive functioning) and our temporal lobe's limbic system (home of the amygdala and the part of our brain that detects danger or safety, assigns emotion, and warehouses our memories). When these regions of the brain are working together well, we feel compassion and joy while simultaneously weighing concerns and tolerating frustration. We can evaluate a perceived threat, stomach the stress of it, be flexible and empathize even when we don't like what we are seeing or hearing. We are open and available for emotional connection with our tween and can repair our connection with them when the signal between us is lost or damaged. We have patience. We are nurturing. When our tween argues or acts offensively, we don't take their behavior personally. We know it's about them, not us, and we are able to stay in their discomfort with them without flying off the handle or retreating.

In contrast, when these regions of the brain are out of sync, we can spiral into frustration, guarded withdrawal, or anger and feel out of control. It is hard for us to sit with our distressed tween. We may focus on our tween's "bad" behavior and disregard the feelings behind their actions. We may take what they say and do personally and overreact. We may criticize, judge, or dismiss them. Most certainly, we will disconnect. Our prefrontal cortex is not helping us tolerate our tween's behavior nor is it helping us manage our emotions. The limbic system is shouting *Danger!* and we react, fast, automatically, as if we really *are* in danger. We can get to the point where our tween walks in the room and we feel our temperature rise as we recall our last interaction and anticipate a repeat of it. Our caregiving system is compromised.

So if our aim is to raise our kids to be resilient, secure, courageous, giving adults—trusting and open to love, *and* we are hardwired to care, to bond, *and* we are motivated and perhaps even have some good tools and a vision of how we want to parent (or *don't* want to parent, like thinking, *I'll never be my parent*), what goes wrong? The inherent caregiver system rooted in our brain structure and function comes from how we were raised and how we have experienced relationships and life in general. We don't know how it all unfolds until we start raising our children and our caregiver system is activated. Enter attachment styles.

The Ways We Attach

Our brain hardwires what we experienced with our parents in our family of origin as we grew up and in other relationships as we moved through school and into adulthood. Our body carries its own version of these memories, because what is recorded in the brain travels throughout the body as a physical reaction. (Remember the autonomic nervous system from Part One: Love Wins. It's got a lot of pull in this body of ours!) When these memories are triggered by current experiences, we access the data associated with them and respond accordingly to the people we love—with trust, responsiveness, play, and joy, or with distrust, distance, anger, and/or nervous energy. What's more, the memories stored in our brain and body combine to become what is called our attachment style. It impacts how we feel, communicate, show love (or not), and raise our children, most often without even realizing it. How we interact with our tween contributes to *their* attachment style.

To understand our attachment style and the reasons for it is to begin to understand the condition of our "soil" and how our past is affecting our parenting, because how we attach constitutes the deepest part of that soil. Once we understand, we can heal; we can change. But first things first:

"Attachment" is another word for the emotional bond that forms between two people.

It is an innate God-given desire. The *way* we *attach* (our style) begins to form when we are born. When we are babies, it is shaped by how safe and protected our parents and caregivers make us feel. As children, our attachment style evolves based on the amount of emotional support and empathy we receive. How our parents bond with us sets the stage for how we find independence and explore our world. It influences our willingness to trust, share our deeper selves, be vulnerable, and give and receive love, ultimately shaping how we pursue love interests and parent our children. The same is happening with our children in how we are bonding with them!

Much of what we know about attachment styles originated in research by psychologists John Bowlby and Mary Ainsworth, who focused on the relationship between infants and their caregiver—ground zero for the formation of our "soil" and any issues that may develop. They discovered that a close bond between parent and infant is essential to a baby's development *and* the baby's ability to have healthy relationships when they grow up.

These early interactions stimulate a child's brain growth, setting the stage for how their brain will process comfort and connection in relationship and understand and manage their emotions when they face adversity. Children pick up on any dysregulation they experience with their parents and mirror these brain structures and behavioral impulses. It's astonishing to think that our child's brain grows and changes based on *our* behavior. For example, children sense a parent's stress and organize around it, often feeling the stress themselves. They then go into the world (school, with peers, extracurricular activities, etc.) with stress hanging over their head. Research has shown us when kids have a difficult time at home, they have trouble learning in school: The brain is functioning to cope with distress, which compromises their ability to concentrate on new concepts and information.

Ainsworth took this theory one step further and named four different attachment styles that emerge as a result of the infant–parent relationship. The tricky thing about understanding these "attachment" styles, though, is this: depending on what we experience in life, beginning with our very first days, our style of attaching could be anything but connecting. Here's how it works.

Secure Attachment Style

Children with a secure attachment style are confident their parent/caregiver will be available when they need them. As infants, they were comforted and protected by a parent/caregiver when they were hungry, in pain, afraid, uncomfortable, startled—any time they were in distress. As their parent responded reliably to their need for safety and security, the parent–child connection deepened. A study from the University of Minnesota showed fourth graders with secure attachment had fewer behavioral problems when their families experienced major stress, such as a death in the family, financial changes, and distress or marital discord, than those who did not. In addition, securely attached children are better at navigating and managing their emotions and behaviors on their own. In other words, they know they have a safety net: A parent is there to comfort them if needed, so they are open to exploring new friendships, activities, and building new skills. They move easily and confidently from one task to another.

Adults with a secure attachment style are available, responsive, and helpful. They have a positive working model of themselves and believe in their ability to make decisions. They are open to taking healthy risks, and they are resilient. They also believe they are worthy of respect, so they tend to shy away from unhealthy relationships. They are emotionally present and willing to receive help and comfort.

Insecure/Avoidant Attachment Style

Adults with an insecure/avoidant attachment style are often described as very independent and hard to get to know. They have not had good experiences with people being there for them when they needed them and may have a deep-rooted perception of parental rejection and criticism left over from when they were kids. That's why they are more apt to avoid intense feelings, intimacy, and conflict: They don't trust anybody. They flee rather than face or fix a problem. They often feel unworthy or unaccepted. They typically become good at self-soothing. They are likely to shy away from relationships, or pull away when they are in them; and when their relationships end, which they inevitably do—a sort of self-fulfilling prophecy—adults with an insecure/avoidant attachment style will feel all the more unworthy, as if something is wrong with them.

Insecure/avoidant attachment style develops in infancy when parents do not respond adequately to a baby's needs: the obvious ones like food and diaper change but also having a routine so they feel well rested, being held close, and responded to when they cry. There is little or no comfort when they are distressed, and they are left feeling alone, in pain, or scared. The infant learns to self-soothe. While self-soothing *is* an important skill, it cannot be a child's only recourse.

In later childhood, kids may develop an insecure/avoidant attachment style if parents are insensitive or critical rather than comforting in times of emotional distress. For instance, a child's feelings are hurt by a friend at school and as they share their pain, their parent cuts them off mid-story, telling them to "Get over it" or "Toughen up." Whether it was their intent or not, the parent rejected the merit of the child's story with their response and left the child feeling not understood and as if something is wrong with them for feeling or thinking the way they did.

Anxious/Ambivalent Attachment Style

An anxious/ambivalent attachment style develops when an infant receives mixed or inconsistent messages from parents. At times, the parent is nurturing. At others, they are distant or insensitive. The infant grows into childhood confused about what to expect from the support figures in their life.

These children may often show signs of anxiety or depression. They have trouble making choices. This leads to uncertainty. Simple questions such as "Are you hungry?" or "Would you like to go to the store with me?" become emotionally disconcerting and hard for them to answer. The frustration of not knowing the "right" answer becomes hard to navigate and leads to emotional outbursts outside the norm for their developmental stage.

Adults with an anxious/ambivalent attachment style typically feel insecure in relationships. They have a negative self-image and see the world through a glass-half-empty lens. They may exhibit exaggerated emotional responses as a way to grab attention or get feedback about how a loved one feels about them or sees them. They may be easy to anger because they expect to be let down, and they often are, which leads to more anger and disappointment when they "allow" it to happen—yet again. They are not good at naming their emotional experiences and regulating their nervous system. In other words, they feel hyped up, hijacked by their emotions, and have a hard time making good behavioral choices that feel good to a child.

Disorganized Attachment Style

We see the disorganized attachment style in adults who have trauma or abuse histories. In infancy, parents are unpredictable and/or abusive, evoking fear and terror. The abuse could be emotional or physical but often leaves an infant feeling afraid, sometimes for their lives.

In childhood, people with disorganized attachment style may long for their caregiver to be safe, so they may try to be close but then fear the pain of being hurt, so they pull away. Children may even dissociate, looking like they are a million miles away, when situations are difficult or emotionally scary. It is as though they are blocking the pain from hitting their consciousness. They would like to flee for safety, but that means leaving their caregiver, which isn't an option for a child.

Adults with disorganized attachment style are difficult to be in relationship with as their behaviors are often unpredictable. Sometimes they seem like they want intimacy, but they may also pull away—petrified of the potential pain if they do get close. To cope with intense emotions, adults with a disorganized attachment style will often disconnect to give themselves a break from the pain or perceived pain that could come from a relationship. For example, they might stop calling or showing up but not say why; they may be reluctant to answer questions about any problem in a relationship and leave it before or just after addressing the issue. They will often come back but with ambivalence and little interest in changing.

This isn't to say if we have a difficult attachment history we are destined to be a bad parent. On the contrary, understanding our attachment tendencies and where they stem from increases our awareness of when and how we show up for our kids. We can see when we are falling into old patterns because of our attachment history but also notice, in the moment, when we are *not* allowing our automatic attachment tendencies to lead us. We will dive into this next when we talk about our soil issues.

ATTACHMENT STYLES AND THEIR ATTRIBUTES

Attachment Style	Secure	Insecure/ Avoidant	Anxious/ Ambivalent	Disorganized
Kids are…	• Confident • Take healthy risks to try new things • Resilient	• Unsure • Suspicious of people's intentions • Learn to self-soothe	• Indecisive • Nervous about making the wrong decisions	• Fearful • Wish for a close parent
Parents are…	• Available • Responsive • Helpful • Present	• Aloof • Independent • Often unavailable emotionally or physically	• Keyed up • Reactive • Unpredictable	• Usually have a history of trauma or abuse, which leaves them unavailable to meet their child's need for boundaries or to be heard and close
How they parent…	• Listen to understand, ask curious questions • Show up during hard times and set boundaries even when it's not fun • Share downtime together; have fun and play	• Use criticism to offer feedback • Insensitive to the pain and hurt of their child's experience	• Miss what their child is saying or feeling • Are overwhelmed by their own emotions • Available at times, randomly	• Exhibit extreme emotions and behaviors that are scary to a child • Rarely available, and when they are it often turns south, leaving the child feeling exposed and vulnerable

CHAPTER TEN

OUR SOIL ISSUES

We have our attachment style based on early exposure to what it felt like to be cared for as an infant and later as we progressed through our childhood and tween years. When a child has a scary experience with a family-of-origin caregiver that leaves them feeling alone, damaged, afraid, and in acute pain, their brain stores it as a significant memory. Therapists call this an attachment injury, and it contributes to our soil issues. While our family-of-origin home life is the primary shaper of our attachment style, our accumulated experiences—good and painful, from academics, extracurriculars, relationships with our peers, our relatives, our teachers, coaches, and others, our young triumphs and defeats, and whatever else may have hit our lives—will also inform how we feel attachment and safety with others, particularly when compounded by trauma.

Though trauma can affect our attachment style, it is separate. A trauma can be a one-time exposure to something frightening that hurts us deeply, such as a tragic death of someone close or being beaten up or abused at school. The death can plant a latent fear of losing others we care about. The abuse can land as fear of going to school each day; worrying about being hurt again can give us an entrenched sense of *I'm not safe. No one can keep me safe.*

Long-term exposure to overt and terrifying trauma, such as growing up with a parent whose gambling addiction costs the family their home, sending them into a transient existence living with a jumble of different relatives, can produce an adult who never feels stable and always worries about money. Similarly, children who live in a community where there is conflict such as gang shootings or drug use can wind up with loads of bedrock in the soil they bring into their adult years.

Then there is covert trauma, such as the child who is told often by a parent they are going to get fat, need to eat certain foods, and stop eating this or that at most of their meals. This child will grow up struggling with their body image and self-worth. Or the child of a parent who repeatedly micromanages their behavior—telling them how to be better, correcting every instance they are wrong, instructing them how and when they should do things—grows up struggling to make decisions, fearing they will fail, so they freeze. They have trouble raising a family and being intimate with their husband or wife.

Over the long haul, trauma and attachment injuries can be lost to our subconscious, but the brain never really lets them go, which is why they can lead to unpredictable emotions, flashbacks, and struggles in relationships. (Not surprisingly, our brain stores trauma and attachment injuries differently than the more accessible happy memories. Think of a vault versus open shelving.)

The brain will recall buried trauma and attachment injuries to the surface of our adult selves when prompted, to prevent them from happening again. So say, for instance, a child watched her parents drink alcohol and argue regularly. A couple of times, the fights escalated to hitting and shoving. One time, it got so bad, she fled to a closet and cried—her parents, with their avoidant parenting, were oblivious to how their behavior affected her. The drinking, yelling, and fighting amounted to an attachment injury for her.

Or perhaps a child's middle school years were filled with such intense bullying that her self-worth vanished as her isolation intensified, sometimes making her wish that she could die so she would no longer have to face it. In high school things turned around as she found friends and the meanness disappeared, along with her tween trauma—so she thought.

Fast forward: The child is now in her twenties. Maybe she's in college or apprenticing to learn a trade or working full-time. Perhaps she is beginning to earn money, pay bills, and cultivate independence as she starts to live on her own. She, like all of us, puts all that childhood stuff in the back of her mind to focus on the here and now. Survival, after all, is right in front of us, demanding our attention. So although we may feel fear, anxiety, depression, worry, and/or inadequacy—stemming from soil issues from our earlier years—we stuff the feelings down to keep our head above water. Most young people in their twenties aren't aware enough to name these emotions at this point in life, let alone understand where they come from. And being young and single, there may not be many people and places reminding us of these soil issues.

So we stay in the dark, through years of dating, sex, and both good and bad relationships. Then kaboom: partner, kids. It's like having our own family awakens the part of us that recalls, consciously or unconsciously, what it was like to be part of a family, have parents, be a kid, to have grown up as we did. The woman, now a mother, looks at her husband drinking alcohol, and her attachment injury awakens to protect her. *Her soil is shifting*: She questions, criticizes, and challenges him in a reaction that is out of proportion to his controlled drinking because she has seen alcohol use go south and is afraid. In her fear, she distances herself from her kids, snapping at them when they ask for something and avoiding their requests for time. She feels overwhelmed. Oxytocin? Dopamine? Forget it. Those hormones couldn't pack their bags fast enough the second her familiar pain resurfaced. The girl-now-a-mom mimics the avoidant style of parenting she experienced as a child. Most likely, she does not consciously know this, nor does she intentionally mean to act as she does. The attachment injury is deeply buried in her brain, yet it is driving her behavior.

And that mom who was bullied as a tween? The second her child experiences even a whiff of what she went through, she panics, freezing up to the point of turning away from it completely. Or she overreacts, making a bigger issue out of what her child may be going through than is warranted, *or* she steps in, ready to fight to "solve" her child's problem. (Not that we should ever allow bullying, but the way to handle it should be driven by *our child's* experience, not *ours*—whether our child is on the giving or receiving end of it.)

We all act in ways powerful and automatic, as memories of what we experienced before in other relationships are triggered. They can be positive, or they can derail our best intentions, compliments of our soil issues—the bruises and injuries of our past that live below the surface, subconsciously imprinted on our way of understanding and behaving in the world. As they appear—in the form of relationship-damaging behavior—we either acknowledge them and work to "remediate our soil" or ignore the problems to the detriment of our "house"—our relationship with our tween and other family members.

The Pain in Our Soil

Attachment injuries and trauma—our soil issues—leave us primarily with one or more of these four pains:

1. **Abandonment:** We are afraid people will leave us, leave us out, or let us go. The fear is so great, we will often try to control people to keep them. We tend to strangle relationships with our need to be together constantly.
2. **Failure:** We've been told so many times we are not doing it right that we fear we will never get it right. We often organize around others and what they want in hope of "getting it right." In the process, we lose our sense of self and what we like, desire, and are interested in.
3. **Shame:** We don't see our value, our worth, so we don't set boundaries, let alone hold to them. We allow others to walk all over us, and we end up feeling very small. Shame leads us to feel defective, unacceptable, unlovable, broken beyond repair.

4. **Fear:** We know bad things can happen and they can change our life in significant ways that will hurt a lot for a long time. We cannot control them or change them. Fear leads us to hold back, not take risks or challenge ourselves because we're afraid of what might happen if we do. We keep our lives small and safe to prevent fear and terror.

One of the questions I get asked the most is "Why did trauma happen to me? Why did I have to go through that? I must be bad and that was the punishment." The truth is, bad things happen to good people. It's a hard concept to grasp when you have experienced such excruciating pain at the hands of someone you trusted, someone who was supposed to love and take care of you. We don't always know why. Even when we do know, it does not make it right or fair. Life takes chunks from us. But we can and will restore what was lost, deepen our relationship with the Holy Spirit within us—that good, God-given place—and find grace toward others in pain.

To parent effectively and fully, the trick is to understand our past so we can recognize what is being triggered now. We must pay attention to the trigger itself, identify it when it rears up, and defang it. It can be hard, though. It's so much easier to avoid seeing the triggers and the feelings of fear, danger, and lack of control that accompany them. So we default to checking off another day…and let the soil issues fester.

However, when we ignore our soil issues and their triggers, we create a vacuum that is filled by automatic behaviors we neither choose nor consciously think much about. (Remember, that clever brain of ours retains *everything*.) When a soil issue is triggered during an interaction with our tween, we will often resist closeness and nurse self-protection quickly and automatically. We may be moody, easily frustrated over small things, reactive, or simply absent. In our denial, we block ourselves from any hope of choosing an emotionally connected behavior such as sitting with our tween, hearing and understanding their frustrations, their joys, their struggles, and their victories.

So know this: When we experience emotions that seem intense, hard to understand, or bigger than what they should be for a given situation, we have likely tapped into pain held from other experiences in our life: a soil issue is being triggered. Here are six common triggers.

Soil Issue Triggers

1. Parenting

Experiences with our own children and tweens will trigger childhood trauma–related soil issues like nothing else in our life. As we covered earlier, trauma in childhood can be one severe event or recurring mild-to-harsh disruptive incidents. Parents may have regularly yelled and fought and not consistently met our basic needs. A childhood home could have lacked a steady caregiver due to alcohol or drugs, divorce, betrayal, death of a loved one, or financial distress. Or the trauma could have been from a bad accident, a broken bone, stitches, a fall from a high chair, or even a difficult birth. In addition to the bullying we discussed earlier in this chapter, it could come from migrating to the United States after living in a refugee camp, being a minority in a hostile dominant culture, frequent change—of homes or schools—or physical, emotional, and/or sexual abuse. Trauma can also happen in the classroom; unsupported learning disabilities can have a profound impact on adulthood.

We grow up from these experiences with a sense of shame, sorrow, and/or fear that lives deep inside us (see sidebar: "The Pain in Our Soil"). Our brain remembers how bad these experiences felt and will try to keep us safe from ever facing them again by reminding us if it ever senses we are in similar "danger." The problem is, sometimes the brain sees a situation as similar and dangerous and propels us into a stress response, yet the situation may not be dangerous at all. For example, a tween starts yelling at the dinner table because she doesn't like an answer to her question about going to a friend's house for a sleepover. Instead of staying calm, the parent's brain has recalled the trauma of sleepovers as a kid in unsafe places and with unsafe people. The parent reacts from this place of fear with a more intense emotion than is warranted by her daughter's simple request.

Because our brain so carefully stores the traumas we may have experienced in our subconscious, typically, we do not think regularly (if at all) about them. Or we may recognize we had a difficult upbringing but don't connect it to how it hurts us in adulthood. In other words, we do not link the here and now to our past: The brain is so efficient, so automatic, it recalls and acts to protect in an instant without conscious awareness. It scans new experiences for similarities to protect against ever feeling that hurt again. It does not go to: *My tween is asking for a sleepover and it reminds me of my scary sleepovers.*

If, during an interaction with our tween, our nervous system registers a similarity to something painful we experienced in childhood, our fight-or-flight stress response system will kick in. When this happens, our brain actually pauses our ability to provide responsive care to our child, defaulting instead to self-protection. Instead of releasing the oxytocin we need to take a step back and actually discuss the sleepover, we get a surge of cortisol, our body's primary stress hormone, and slam shut the door on our tween. In this state, we are blinded to the pain and confusion that may be driving our tween's behavior. Rather, we see our tween as rude, abusive, egocentric, disrespectful, and inappropriate. We may describe them as depressed, anxious, demanding, or dismissive of the family. We blame the problems we are having on them. It spares us from addressing any deep hurt we may be feeling, the soil issue we've surfaced. Some parents don't realize this is happening, while others may know it but are unwilling to acknowledge it or don't know how to deal with it. Additionally, some children may trigger us more than others; that's why parenting one child can feel so different from parenting another.

Although our tween's behavior may warrant intervention and boundaries, when we are blocked by a soil issue, the *way* we choose to intervene will most likely harm our connection with them. Tweens do not understand any underlying feelings we may be having; they interpret what they hear in the deeply egocentric way of their developmental stage, taking away messages such as, *My parents don't like me*, or *I'm not doing a good job*, or *Maybe my family would be better off without me*, and, above all, *My parents don't understand me.*

Over time, our tween will stop reaching out to us if we do not understand their emotional pain. They will start to feel, innately, that we are not safe, because they do not understand our overreactions. To protect themselves, tweens withdraw and avoid us, maintain a defensive wall, or argue or become aggressive toward us.

Ideally, we will notice the familiar feelings and link them to our soil issue. When we understand our family-of-origin wounds and childhood traumas and recognize when they are triggered, we can find the grace to slow down and make more intentional choices in how we respond to our tweens. This also trains our brain to stay calm and eliminate the release of cortisol. We will talk more about this in the next part when we cover remediating our soil issues.

2. Partner Discord

We know human connection is vital to our mental, emotional, and physical health. So it may not surprise you to learn that the essential element of a healthy relationship between partners is actually not the way couples work together, or their common interests, opinions, or traits. Rather, the essential element of a healthy relationship is based on a couple's ability to be emotionally responsive to each other, to connect. When we feel connected and close, seen and heard, understood and supported in partner relationships, we are healthier and better able to concentrate. We have more energy and challenge ourselves in positive ways. We draw strength from our partner relationship.

Conversely, when we feel disconnected from our partner, our blood pressure rises along with our level of stress hormones. The distance can leave us feeling lonely, unseen, and rejected. Our relationship can feel unreliable and unsafe. We can become distracted, unbalanced, depressed, or anxious. Conflict-laden or overly critical partnerships increase self-doubt and lower self-esteem.

Plainly, our partner relationship holds a lot of weight inside our heart, mind, and body. That is why a friend or coworker cannot make us nearly so mad as our partner can.

When two people become parents, the way each was parented and the soil issues associated with each one's experience will soon collide. Virtually no one escapes this. Stressors such as buying a house, finances, and budgeting, individual obstacles such as building a career, being a new parent, taking care of parents as they age can all challenge the relationship even further. Partners may start to drift, an ebbing of connection. It may seem minor at first glance, a misunderstanding, but it can compound, like boats at sea. We mean to stay close but the flow of the water pulls us in different directions, slowly, inexorably. Before we realize it, we are miles apart, and it hurts.

As partners drift, missing their former friendship and longing to be heard and understood as they once were, the pain can escalate. To escape the hurt, partners either withdraw or fight. So now the relationship is triggering a stress response, which presents as blaming, nagging, arguing, criticizing, or silence, avoidance, coolness: *I miss you* is lost beneath it all.

If partners are filled with resentment and/or pain and the worry that comes with their distressed relationship, it is hard to parent with an open, comforting, and responsive heart. The heart is frightened and fragile! It is difficult for it to be afraid in one relationship in the home and calm and soothing in another.

Furthermore, tweens pick up on parent discord and conflict. They may use it to their advantage by playing one parent against the other or siding with the parent they can get more from. They may also worry that the parent discord will impact their safety and security, which can distract them from school and other responsibilities.

In fact, the whole family system will suffer. Parents distracted by the pain they provoke in each other may be short-tempered with their kids, complain about each other to their kids, or withdraw from the entire family. Tweens, especially, may feel the lack of security in their parents' relationship and ask for reassurance through whining, arguing, or blaming one parent. What they are really saying in their ill-equipped way is: *Am I safe? Do you love me?* (Remember, the tween brain does not yet know how to communicate tough stuff.)

Take an inventory of your marriage and see if you can discern what your tween is exposed to. Are you your best self? Does your partnership build you up or pull you down? What are you and your partner modeling for your kids? If you are struggling, talk to a couples' therapist and see if you can heal some of the relational issues between you. You will feel better, and your kids will see happy, healthy parents whom they can look up to and trust as they enter their teen years. You will also model the type of relationship they will seek in their future.

3. Distress

There are two kinds of stress: eustress and distress. Eustress causes mild anxiety or low-grade stress, the kind that gets us moving, alert. It typically gives us the gusto to stop procrastinating and get to it. Distress is what hurts and worries us. It can be distracting, slow us down, or block the way forward entirely. Eustress we need. Distress can be a trigger.

Current painful experiences such as job loss, work stress, divorce, financial crisis, death, medical problems, or the hormonal changes common with aging are the kinds of distress that can dramatically impact our ability to understand and respond to our tween's needs. These might be one-time incidents with a long-term aftermath or an ever-present difficult situation.

When we are in the midst of a painful adult experience, it changes the way we feel and see the world. We have intense emotions draining and depleting us, and in the aftermath of tragedy, we may struggle to express our emotions when they surface. Physical pain can have a huge impact on how we feel about ourselves, our future, and the possibilities available to us. We may have a difficult time thinking. We may be tired and mentally unavailable for our tweens; depression, anxiety, or temper may override our ability to parent responsively. An otherwise harmonious relationship with our tween can become troubled.

At times like this, we are more sensitive to conflict and the behavior of others. Our tween can trigger our feelings by talking loudly or too fast, using disrespectful language, being disorganized, making a mess around the house, and more. Although they are not doing any of this to *us*, the fact that it is happening when we are depleted and distressed makes our reaction more intense. Sometimes we may yell. Other times, we may not respond, because we just don't have the energy.

When we're involved or thinking about these painful experiences, our tween—many for the first time—may feel we're unavailable or not helpful. Because tweens may not understand how to interpret our new demeanor, they will most often take our reaction personally, mistakenly thinking we don't care about them, we are mad at them, or we just don't like them.

Our tween may behave in one of three ways during these stressful times.

- They could be dutiful and obedient in hope of being seen as a "good kid" and feeling a renewed connection with us.
- They may act out to protest the pain of not knowing what happened to change us.
- They may withdraw, staying away from us in the hope they will be off the radar and not do anything "wrong" to anger us.

In all of these scenarios, our tween is indicating they notice something changed, they miss us and want to be close again.

We must recognize that in times of stress, our emotions affect our tween. We should try to talk about our distress, when possible, and not simply lash out or avoid them, particularly when our acting out is from a place of discomfort within ourselves. And if we do find ourselves expressing unfamiliar emotions and disconnecting with our tween, we can repair the connection with developmentally appropriate conversations about what happened and why. An open dialogue helps both parents and tweens understand changes are not anyone's fault. It also reassures our tween they have not done anything wrong and we still love them.

Above all, we must convey to them that we are still here and love them. Just saying the words will bring a sense of relief and reassurance to our tween. As parents, we will have a bad moment—we all experience them, and sometimes they last months or even years. It's how we model our emotions that matters most, both for ourselves and for our relationship with our tween.

4. Developmental Changes

Most parents can quickly recall the hardest developmental stage to parent. It's universal: We relate to our kids more at certain stages and have a harder time connecting at others. Negotiating rules and boundaries with a teenager can take more energy for some parents than the tantrums of a two-year-old. Others don't like the noise and chaos of a young child in the house. Parents can have a difficult time understanding their behavior or what they need. These challenging times can produce emotional reactions in us that affect our ability to show up for our kids. We may feel defensive, confused, frustrated, or defeated and struggle with outbursts because we are holding so much in as we try to do the right thing. We may wish to escape or feel frustrated and think: *Why is he acting like that?* or *She's behaving that way on purpose just to make me mad.* Sometimes we put it on ourselves: *Why can't I help my child feel better?* or *If only I had intervened earlier…*

A good way to handle these feelings is to recognize that some stages of development just make more sense to us than others. It's okay! We can remind ourselves we didn't act this way or our family wasn't like this. This is new behavior, and the unknown of this stage makes us uneasy. We may feel uncertain and off balance, and may default to trying to over-control or react in a way that isn't healthy. Such self-awareness frees us from denial and opens the way to think differently. (*Much* more to come on this in Part Four: Remediating Our Soil.)

5. Tweens with Special Needs

When our tween is diagnosed with a chronic medical issue, a learning disability, or a mental health disorder, or if there is adoption trauma or any number of other unique circumstances requiring more time, resources, understanding, patience, and education, we must be a parent not only to our child's emotional needs but to their special needs as well.

Children quickly learn they have special challenges as the message *you are different* is reinforced by doctors, parents, teachers, and therapists (unintended as this may be). They compare themselves to their peers and see how they measure up. This can be especially difficult for tweens due to their newfound sensitivity to their peers. As you will recall from Part Two: It's Not You, It's Neuroscience, conformity and measuring up are so important at this stage. When tweens feel "less than" or "other," their self-worth can take a hit. Tweens with special needs can also develop a negative self-belief when they can't fix the problems they struggle with.

Special needs can drive tweens to impulsive, provocative, and challenging behaviors and extreme feelings of rejection, hurt, inadequacy, and anxiety. So not only is the special need unique, but there are also the behaviors and emotions that accompany it.

We want to offer the best solutions to make life easier for our tween and give them as normal a childhood as possible. Parents are often filled with sadness, watching their children struggle and seeing their sudden anger, usually from the stress of holding everything together or feeling like a failure. We may overcompensate to show our love, giving our tween more or by not setting healthy boundaries. Parents can park in denial and figure it will get better rather than have difficult conversations or hear tough information about their child.

Even though parents and tweens have the same goals, there is a strain on the interaction between parent and child. Parents often feel powerless and focus on the fix, leaving their tween feeling more like a project than a child. Parents can hyper-focus on intervention and advice in hope of making the problem go away, which leaves the tween feeling pressure and anxious to get it right.

In truth, there may be a limit to how much we can do. Sometimes we just have to surrender. Instead of changing or fixing it, never underestimate the power of sitting in it with our child and learning from them: Where there is hardship and challenge, there can also be great reward. Children with special needs tell us this—in their fight, their spirit, and all that makes them the unique individuals they are. There is no greater teacher of true love and perspective. As our faith teachings tell us, the least among us shall be the greatest and the meek shall inherit the earth. We need only look to find the joy, and peace.

6. Untreated* Addiction and Mental Illness

Addiction comes in many forms: the obvious—drugs, alcohol, gaming, pornography, social media, and shopping—and the not-so-obvious—working, over-functioning, and perfectionism. Addiction is any behavior we use regularly to feel better or mask unhappy feelings. And there's just no way around it: Untreated addiction or mental illness has a profound effect on our personal wellness, relationships, and on our parenting. It can tear families apart.

When we are actively using something to feel better, two big things are happening:

1. We are unable to see our tween and empathize with their pain. Addictions dim our ability to pick up on the cues our tween may be sending to us for emotional support.

2. We are unable to feel fully ourselves, which means we lose our authenticity to parent from a loving and nurturing place.

In our interactions with our tween, we are often moody and at the mercy of how we feel based on our untreated and active illness. We are inconsistent and impulsive, which makes it difficult for our tween to understand us. Our tween will see the negative impact of our excessive behavior

---

* When I say "untreated," I mean there are no professional support or preventative lifestyle choices in place to counter the addiction or minimize the risk factors that lead to episodes of mental illness.

on our life and question if they can trust us with their secrets, or look to us as role models. They cannot rely on us to be there for them in a meaningful way. They know we will let them down. They learn to guard their heart from us and take care of their own needs, either by themselves or by finding others to take our place. This can leave them hard to bond with. To them, people aren't safe, and they tend to escape their pain through negative self-talk and self-destructive behaviors of their own.

Spotting Addiction: When a Behavior Is a Problem

- It is impacting the time you spend with the people and things you enjoy most.

- It is keeping you from meaningful family time.

- It is causing you to think and do things that are not your best self.

- After engaging in it, you don't feel fulfilled.

- It is stopping you from growing, learning, feeling inspired and creative.

- It is affecting your sleep.

Untreated mental illness carries a similar wrecking ball to our relationship with our tween. At a minimum, untreated mental illness keeps us from being present with them. Complicating matters, anxiety, depression, and other forms of mental illness suppress our brain's ability to feel empathy. During active episodes, the very idea of nurturing flies out the window, separating us even further from our tween.

Our tween may also see us as moody, depressed, anxious, judgmental, or unhappy. They may register our anger as directed at them and feel bad about themselves. Furthermore, our erratic behavior—isolating ourselves, sleeping at strange times, sleeping too much, over-exercising, obsessively dieting, failing to show up, explosive outbursts, and more—will make them feel unsafe in their home environment and lead to problem behaviors of their own. Tweens with parents who suffer from untreated mental illness may express depressive symptoms, have lower self-esteem, forfeit activities they enjoy while they care for the parent and fill parenting roles such as cooking meals and caring for siblings.

You Are Not Alone

People who are diagnosed with depression, anxiety, bipolar disorder, etc., are dealing with real symptoms. The symptoms can be better or worse depending on environmental circumstances, medication management, and lifestyle choices. It is crucial that mental health issues are honestly treated and cared for. There is no shame in having a mental health issue: approximately 8.3 million adults in the U.S. alone suffer from some form of mental health disorder. There is no need to fight it alone. If you are ready to receive help, call 1-800-273-TALK for twenty-four-hour referral services. You can also reach out to your employee assistance program if your employer offers one, your insurance company for in-network behavioral health providers, and 911 if you are at risk of hurting yourself or someone else.

It is one thing to stop a behavior, but it is quite another thing to heal. Adults will white-knuckle as they try to stop an addictive behavior, but if they don't explore their "soil issues" and learn why they developed the addiction in the first place and what triggers it, they will deprive themselves of a critical helping hand, and it will be nearly impossible to truly recover. They must do the hard work of AA, treatment, therapy, medication, inpatient, Intensive Out Patient (IOP), etc., to learn, to grow, to practice compassion for themselves and reclaim their lives.

Tween Behaviors When the Home Environment Is Unsafe

- Whining, having a lot of needs that never seem to be met.

- Complaining, criticizing out of frustration they cannot explain.

- Taking on adultlike responsibilities such as cooking and caring for siblings.

- Giving up activities they used to like because they are anxious about leaving the house.

- Stop sharing their ideas, thoughts, and feelings.

- Their childlike qualities seem to dim.

Moving Forward

Do you see the parts of yourself that are confident, thriving, resilient, strong, and longing to connect with your tween? Do you see the parts that are insecure, anxious, fearful, or easily irritated? You now know why: They come from our soil, the foundation upon which we build the relationships in our lives. It starts with the attachment style that began forming when we were born and continues to evolve even now. And with that soil come issues for everyone, and they impact how we behave toward the people close to us and shape how we parent.

But we *can* remediate our soil—get rid of the bedrock, resolve the contamination, and drain the water. We were not created to live in darkness long term. Our faith teachings tell us that time and time again. Each of us is fashioned with amazing strengths and gifts—a bright spirit meant to thrive and live in community with others. All of this is about identifying what I think of as our God-given path. Everyone has a path, and sometimes we are asked to do hard stuff to find it, or regain it when we lose our way: Understanding ourselves is the first step toward that, and every step we take also brings us closer to our tween.

QUESTIONS TO PONDER

1. What attachment style do you identify with from your childhood?

2. Are there scenarios that trigger your soil issues?

3. If you wrote a paragraph about your soil issue, what would you say?

PART FOUR

Remediating Our Soil

Healing Ourselves to Connect with Our Tween

"We project our terror on our children and store the pain in our body. To reclaim our life and conscious parenting we reparent ourselves to be the parent we never had. We become aware of the moves of our inner child and comfort self."

—SHEFALI TSABARY, CLINICAL PSYCHOLOGIST, EXPERT IN FAMILY DYNAMICS AND PERSONAL DEVELOPMENT

"A farmer went out to sow his seed. As he was scattering the seed, some fell along the path; it was trampled on, and the birds ate it up. Some fell on rocky ground, and when it came up, the plants withered because they had no moisture. Other seed fell among thorns, which grew up with it and choked the plants. Still other seed fell on good soil. It came up and yielded a crop, a hundred times more than was sown."

—LUKE 8:5–15 NIV

In the last chapter, we uncovered how the deeper parts of ourselves—our soil issues—can block the way to our tween. But they don't have to. We *can* clear the path. This part explains how.

As you have read, soil issues come from our attachment style—how we were parented. This shaped the structure and functioning of our brain and ultimately drives how we parent our own children. Soil issues also come from other childhood experiences that left us in pain: traumatic things that happened to us in school, our neighborhood, in sports, with our parents, with other adults, or in other parts of our younger years.

Such childhood experiences are triggered in the present by a whole range of scenarios. If we think that distressing experience from our childhood was a long time ago and doesn't affect us now, think again. It's sometimes surprising to learn just how much it may be impacting our life and relationships today. As we discussed in Part Three: What Lies Beneath, spotting it is the first step toward loosening its hold on us.

Digging into our soil issues—those places within us that are filled with unresolved pain—can be heavy, hard work, leaving us feeling drained and exposed. However, it is how we close the divide that may exist between us and our tween, and it is well worth the effort. Because even though we never mean to disconnect from our tween and *swear we will do better next time* after each disagreement, until we understand and resolve our soil issues, the arguments will persist, and we will continue to miss opportunities to connect. So welcome to the ways we can "remediate our soil," heal and clear the way to building emotional connection with our tween. It may seem impossible to change—these are, after all, ingrained patterns in our brain that we are dealing with. But, while change may not be easy, it is important to remember *it is always possible.*

Indicators help us along the way, what I think of as "winks from God." Some think of them as coincidences. Whatever we call them, these are signals we are on the right path and not alone. Wherever we may be on the faith spectrum, the transforming love of Christ is available to everyone. We all have the Holy Spirit in us, giving us power and direction, no matter how we may process it. It shines bright when we are on the right path.

We can feel it in our gut. We have clarity in our decisions and life choices. We are stronger and give more to our relationships. It's how we get to "the good soil."

Changing Our Legacy

Our childhood experiences and the attachment style we developed as a result of how our parents raised us affect how we are able to connect (or not) with our tween. If we have unresolved pain, we can feel adrift and question our parenting or misread the motives behind our tween's actions. A tween will pick up on the uncertainty and disconnect between us. It shapes the structure and functioning of their brain, just as our experiences with our parents shaped ours. They will carry it into their lives and their own parenting (just as we did). So, it is important that we heal ourselves to keep from passing our "chalice of pain" from one generation to another.

That same Power nudges us to do the hard things—to remediate our soil and get to those winks. If we are open to them, we can actually feel them, just as we can see the winks. As we remediate our soil, keep in mind that sometimes our darkest moments are for a bigger purpose, one we cannot possibly understand when we are in the midst of them. Only as we work through them can we begin to see the winks, and that starts with compassion...*self*-compassion.

CHAPTER ELEVEN

START WITH COMPASSION...
FOR YOURSELF

Perfection does not exist. Let me repeat: Perfection does not exist. When it comes to our friends and family, we are quick to reinforce this and give them the sensitivity and compassion we rarely (if ever) think to extend to ourselves. Yet when it comes to dealing with our own pain, suffering, anxiety, and insecurities, self-compassion is essential. God calls us to this. There are no prerequisites for the unconditional—and therefore, strengthening—love He extends to us; we must give *ourselves* the forgiveness and compassion we *receive*. Self-compassion obliges us to see our personal struggles through a lens of kindness. With kindness to self, we open ourselves to breaking the cycle of self-induced pain; we open ourselves to healing. It sets the stage for remediating our soil.

According to Kristen Neff, PhD, one of the world's leading experts on self-compassion, self-compassion means:

- Not criticizing or judging ourselves
- Giving ourselves kindness and self-care
- Honoring who we are and granting ourselves permission to love our messy imperfections as well as the parts that are beautiful, capable, and deserving

- Knowing we are not alone; people want to be "in it" with us (God wants to be in it with us!)
- Being mindful of our negative thoughts and accepting that they exist without letting them take over and drive our emotions and actions.

How to Develop Self-Compassion

1. Acknowledge yourself through a lens of kindness.

Most of us are the last to see our own suffering for what it really is. We avoid it, try to sugarcoat it, and sidestep people who make us feel pain. We criticize ourselves with negative self-talk that can descend into feelings of embarrassment, inadequacy, and shame. Or we judge and blame ourselves for not being able to *Do more!, Be better!, Act differently!* We may also deny the presence of our pain, thinking that we are alleviating whatever is making us feel bad by erasing it. (This *never* works.) Or, if we do manage to acknowledge our pain, we may minimize it and push ourselves to *Snap out of it!*

No one can change if they are beating themselves up, falling through a shame spiral, or just going through the motions of life trying to do the right thing. There's no path forward, no way to examine ourselves or our past and connect it to how it may be affecting our parenting. We *must* start with a kind inner voice. When our inner voice is on our side, it becomes our nurturer when we fall, our champion in our triumphs, and our cheerleader in our challenges, pushing us outside our comfort zone to tackle our soil issues and the tough situations that come our way.

Often, we also think we're uniquely flawed and alone in what we are feeling. *We are not.* If anyone says otherwise, they are lying. With the acknowledgment part of self-compassion, we recognize that our distress, suffering, self-doubt, wishing we had done better, and even our failures are universally human.

Self-Esteem vs. Self-Compassion

Self-compassion is different from self-esteem. Sometimes we confuse the two. Self-esteem is a personal, subjective measurement of how we see our worth and value in the world. Usually it requires us to judge ourselves against others to determine how "good" we are. Self-compassion, on the other hand, is not a measurement of self-worth but more a practice of care, kindness, and understanding toward self during times of distress.

Self-Compassion	Self-Esteem
We relate to self with a sense of rightness in who we are in the moment, regardless of how things are going.	We evaluate ourselves as good, right, enough…or not.
Based on kindness toward self and the knowledge that all humans struggle.	Based on how we see ourselves in comparison to others.
Offers space to feel empathy for ourselves and others during times of trial.	Leaves us on an emotional roller coaster of having to be better or feel better than someone or something.
Feel connected or part of something bigger than ourselves.	Feel isolated or separate.
Focus is on caring for self, relationships, and other people.	Focus is on being better in what we do, often harsh and critical of self.
Usually has a more emotionally stable sense of worth.	Usually more excited when feeling good about self and has a bigger drop when feeling less than others.
Tend to take more responsibility for behaviors; open to change.	Tend to blame others for our deficits, mishaps, or disappointments.

When we do this, we honor the part of us that is hurting and give ourselves kindness instead of pushing harder, beating ourselves up, or avoiding our pain altogether. This silences that punishing inner voice and opens the door to patience and grace, and the healing and new possibilities that come with them.

I once had a client who got such terrible migraines that she would end up in bed for two days. We traced them to the unrealistically high bar she set for herself in all things: She would drive herself ruthlessly, overbooking herself, never taking a break and cutting deeply into her sleep time. She did not share her feelings with others or even acknowledge her feelings most of the time. Instead, she would get mad at herself for being exhausted, failing to keep up with others, and not holding it together better.

As she examined herself through a lens of self-compassion, she recognized she wasn't seeing her struggles as a part that deserved attention, patience, and love. She saw she was treating herself with a cruelty to which she would *never* subject friends or family during *their* painful times. The migraines were her body finally hitting her over the head (literally!) and saying: *This is too much!*

Once she allowed herself kinder self-reflection, she was able to acknowledge why she was getting migraines. She could see she was bound to make mistakes and struggle with things that seemed easy for others. We all do! She was able to accept this as part of the human experience, give herself a break, and work on catching the early signs of her distress so that she could intervene with self-care before the migraine took hold.

2. You're not flying solo.

Allowing others to hear our frustration and help us is one of the best kinds of self-care. We feel heard. We feel understood. We give ourselves the opportunity to see how others have similar experiences, feelings, and distress. We realize we really *can* handle the hard stuff. If we fall down, we can get back up: Our people will be there rooting for us. What's more, all

The Best Kind

From the silly to the sublime, the things we can do to extend kindness to ourselves are just about *anything* that makes us feel better. They can cost time, they can cost money, they can cost nothing. Here are some thoughts to get you started on coming up with self-care for yourself. Remember, a little care can go a long way.

- Dance…in the kitchen, in the backyard, wherever you want.
- Create a favorite space in your home.
- Take a nap.
- Sing.
- Go to bed earlier and get up early.
- Stop and listen to the quiet.
- Skip alcohol on weekdays; try even on weekends.
- Eat that favorite meal.
- Splurge on dessert.
- Take time to talk to friends.
- Exercise how you want.
- Journal.
- Make time for downtime.
- Find your playful side and let it fly.
- Accept help.
- Get a massage, a haircut, a pedicure or manicure.
- Do that thing you keep meaning to do: Read that book, listen to that podcast, take that class, clean out that closet.

this outside support helps us find the guts to dig deeper to learn why we react as strongly as we do to certain triggers.

When my client with the migraines examined what was going on in her life before each migraine hit her, she spotted a number of triggers: She felt defeated at work by a boss who wouldn't promote her. She wouldn't talk about it with her husband yet she would become irritated with him for not reading her mind and being with her in her pain. She wouldn't talk *to anyone* about it. Instead, she bottled up all her anxiety and created stress that was compounded by the daily demands of her life.

Once aware of this, she began to stop herself, sit in her discomfort, name her feelings, and really look at what was making her feel the way she did. She then spent time extending care and kindness to herself *before* the migraine started. She reminded herself that her disappointment over not getting the promotion and feeling alone in the experience were common. She went out with friends, gave herself downtime on weekends. Most importantly, she shared her distress with her husband.

3. Be present in the moment.

I'm talking about mindfulness here, and it too is a key part of developing the self-compassion we need to address our soil issues. Mindfulness is about dropping in on the exact moment we are in, noticing the world around us and our place in it. It allows us to see our self in unique moments, which is how we are able to move from the aimlessness of "just getting through the day" to the intentionality necessary for productive change.

When we see life as individual moments, we appreciate the subtlety of our experiences and connections in our relationships. We understand ourselves, our feelings, and emotions with a sharpness that doesn't exist when we are running through life on autopilot.

Mindfulness strips the worry from us about the past or what is yet to come. *It is our path to perspective.* It also gives us opportunities to practice not overidentifying with our pain. When we overidentify, we feel shame and shut down or project our feelings onto others, (like our tween). We may react in ways that make us feel worse, creating a cycle of escalating self-induced pain. Mindfulness breaks this corkscrew, allowing us to separate our disappointment from our pain so that it does not define us. This also gives us a chance to choose a more thoughtful, kinder response to ourselves and others.

Mindfulness is as simple as noticing how our child's voice makes our heart warm when they walk in the house and call out, "Mom" or "Dad." When we are mindful, we can more easily see the things for which we can be grateful…and gratitude is among the best raw materials I know for building self-compassion.

Mindfulness opens our eyes to the things that trigger the pain we carry—the way someone responds to us, a particular social setting, or something someone says or does. It gives us the awareness we need to link the triggers to the parts of our past that are causing distress—that is, our soil issues—and observe how this distress is impacting our mood and behavior. It gives us a way to control our response, because when we are mindful, we can catch our emotions the moment we feel them.

With mindfulness, we have the clarity and objectivity to see a situation in its true context and stop any unrelated (but triggered nonetheless) soil-issue reactions. For example, with our tween, if their expression is sour or their tone is abrasive, do we tense up? Turn off? Do we see their behavior as something they are "doing to us"? Mindfulness lets us see they are having an emotional experience that could be caused by a variety of things, none of which have anything to do with us or our past. Perhaps that abrasive tone is related to something that happened at school. Or maybe our tween is just hungry, thus the sour look. When we are mindful, we can choose our reaction with the intention and empathy that will connect us emotionally.

Mindfulness also allows us to catch ourselves in the moment *our tween* disconnects from *us* in reaction to something we said. This gives us the opportunity to stop the break in its tracks, because when we are mindful, we are quicker to intervene when something doesn't feel good or when others are hurting.

When we are mindful, we tend to talk about things that bother us rather than hold on to feelings and let them build inside us.

Beware the Pressure Cooker

Like a pressure cooker, when we hold in our feelings, they will blow in some way. Maybe not the first time, or the second, or even the third. But at some point, they will demand release, and when they do, don't be surprised when the room clears and your tween shuts down, confused by what appears to them as a sudden, surprising reaction to something that seemed never to affect us before. Another way our feelings can "blow" is by escalating into bigger emotions that can be more problematic. For instance, anxiety can become panic, sadness can become emptiness, and anger or rejection can intensify to feeling abandoned.

When we reduce this ruminating distress, we create neural pathways of positive thinking and confident self-talk. (This positions us to catch those winks.) We feel empowered, lighter. Mindfulness benefits our physical health as well: When we don't bury our feelings, we lower inflammation and improve our immune health.

Mindfulness also builds our resilience and compassion. It connects us to all the things that make us who we are. *All* parts of us need to be acknowledged and understood, and all parts of us can and should have a presence in our behaviors toward ourselves and our tween. To embrace what we like about ourselves and put our soil issues in their proper perspective, stripping them of their influence on our behaviors, is to give ourselves space to address what is throwing our relationships out of whack.

This is where self-compassion becomes action—a willingness to learn about ourselves and grow into the feelings and ways we see ourselves in the world through this new knowledge. It is at the root of how we change the way we act toward others.

Be Willing to Grow

If we are willing to learn about ourselves through the lens of self-compassion, we *will* grow. It begins with a willingness to do hard things. Remember those nudges we spoke of earlier? That is God steering us in meaningful and important directions. Sometimes they are really difficult—like stepping back to examine how our past experiences and relationships (with our family, friends, children, and others) might be shaping our feelings and behaviors. Sometimes the direction has an expense we don't think we can afford, such as attending an educational group, going to rehab, or finding a therapist who will partner with us in the process of change. And sometimes the steps required to heed the nudge feel too time-consuming and we're stretched too thin already to fit them in our packed days. The truth is, God will make the time, money, and motivation available to us. We just need to follow the nudge. Is it easy? No. Will we feel amazing on the other side of it? Yes. Will our relationships be stronger? No question!

This gives us a way to productively own our thoughts and actions, and make better choices in how we behave in our relationships. It makes each of us a better person and a better parent.

As positive as the upside is to of all this, I find it is generally the last place parents will go when they come to me because of "problems" they are having with their tween. In fact, parents will often bring their tween to me "to fix." I take one look and see that the problem is with the relationship between the parents, *not* the tween! But *they* won't go into therapy; they put their *tween* in therapy.

Most people dodge learning about themselves because it's hard. They also feel (mistakenly) it won't change anything. Primarily, it's because when they approach the mirror to examine themselves, the dark places from unresolved soil issues reflect back at them, and they feel shame. Most of us have at least one dark place…that part that calls to us, saying—*I am a bad person, I am incompetent, I will never get it right, I will never measure up no matter what I do, No one will ever love me if they really know me,* or *I am a failure.* And when parents camp in these darkest places, they tend to blame their tween for any difficulty they may be having with the relationship. It's easier than looking inside themselves to discern the real source of the problem.

However, there is a light switch, a way to get rid of the darkness. The key is taking the shame out of it.

Empathy, the Shame Slayer

Best-selling author and guru of courage, vulnerability, shame, and empathy Brené Brown tells us shame is the most powerful of all our emotions. It is the voice inside that says *I'm not good enough.* It is different from guilt, which is about a particular circumstance. Shame is all-encompassing. When we see ourselves through a shame lens, we lose our perspective, our ability to rationally see a situation. It becomes all or nothing, a sort of *I have to change everything* or *I have to quit.* We cannot shame someone into changing their behaviors. Ironically, when we try, it only cements the inability to change by reinforcing the shame. Conversely, empathy slaughters shame. If we can share our story with an empathetic friend or family member, shame can't survive.

When we stop blaming ourselves and our kids for the strife we may be experiencing and make the effort to learn the truth about our deeper self, we can grow to a new, more connected place of parenting.

The common thread in all we've covered so far in this chapter is self-awareness—from self-compassion—including acknowledging yourself through a lens of kindness, seeking help, and being mindful, to a willingness to learn about yourself and be open to growing wiser and stronger—to be a better friend and better parent.

Without self-awareness:

- We cannot know what we are feeling.
- We cannot see our soil issues.
- We cannot learn.
- We cannot change.

With self-awareness, there's truly nothing we can't handle and no relationship we cannot build with our tween. It is the way we develop the ability to respond intentionally rather than reactively in all our relationships.

CHAPTER TWELVE

HEALING THROUGH SELF-AWARENESS

Self-awareness is the ability to have an honest and accurate perspective of our life, our behavior, and all that makes us who we are. This means:

- Understanding our past experiences, relationships, and the meaning we attach to them.
- Pinpointing the thoughts and feelings that trace back to past experiences.
- Identifying what we're feeling in our here-and-now interactions.
- Teasing out the difference between what we wish was true and what is true.
- Recognizing our strengths, weaknesses, personal values, pain, triggers, and responses.

Self-awareness is not how we think we look in the eyes of others. It has nothing to do with what others say or how they treat us. If after an interaction with someone close to us we feel mad, sad, impatient, or any other emotion that does not feel good, rather than zeroing in on *their* behavior, self-awareness calls us to look within *ourselves* to explore what is truly motivating our response.

We use kindness to open up that inner Pandora's box we all have. It is loaded with our feelings and memories—the key to understanding our reactions to here-and-now experiences. Self-awareness helps us examine what's inside honestly. Self-awareness is how we make sense of ourselves. It is the difference between *Oh, she said that and it made me mad. What makes her think it's appropriate to say that out loud?* and *Boy, when she said that, it tapped into my insecurity and made me question how I was speaking. Truth be told, I think I was being open, sharing something important, and it just wasn't well-received.* Our ability to be self-aware is dependent on our capacity to slow down, look inside ourselves, and see what is really happening for us in the moment it is occurring. It is the inner workings of mindfulness, where the world around us intersects with our thoughts and emotions.

How to Strengthen Your Ability to Be Self-Aware

1. Read your body.

Our body can tell us what we are feeling, if we pay attention, because we experience emotion physically. Our physical reactions are among the best translators we have for what is going on inside our brain. They are a front-row seat to self-awareness. You may think you're not reacting but look closer: Are your neck or shoulders tense? Perhaps you feel knots, butterflies, or a pit in your stomach, a lump in your throat, or an adrenaline rush of energy. Maybe your arms go numb, you get a headache, or your heart pounds. What does your facial expression look like to others? Perhaps you feel a sudden urge to catch your breath and can't. Maybe you sweat, or your eyes may widen, fill with tears, or you may close them entirely, bracing for an interaction something deep inside has conditioned you to expect will ooze pain. When this happens during an exchange with your tween, slow down and pace yourself. Allow yourself time to process what is going on in your *right here, right now.* It's okay to take a minute or two. It's okay to ask for a five-minute reset to "go to the bathroom" and then return to your tween. Or, if you need more time to sit in self-awareness, let your tween know you want to regroup and talk again later. (Just be sure to set a specific time.)

The Mind–Body Connection

Emotion	Physical Reaction
Abandoned	Negative thinking, empty, holding back tears
Anger, frustration	Feeling warm, headache, flushed face, shoulder tension, tense in posture, thoughts racing, rising blood pressure
Anxiety	Racing thoughts, can't sit still or can't concentrate, neck and shoulder tension, chest tightening
Disappointment	Tired
Failure	Small; we actually appear smaller in the mirror; failure changes our self-image
Fear	Racing or foggy thoughts, indigestion, constipation, numbness in the arms
Inadequacy	Itchy, cold
Rejection	Empty
Sadness	Lump in throat, low energy, tears
Shame	Empty, small, low
Taken advantage of	Tightness in muscles

2. Name the feeling.

Once we are aware of what is happening in our body, and we divert our focus from what other people (including our tween) may be saying or doing to us, we can attach feelings to our response.

For instance, anxiety often comes with racing thoughts of "what if" scenarios, chest tightening, neck and shoulder tension, or trouble concentrating or finishing a task. The discomfort can be mild and last an hour or distracting and last through an evening. If we cannot make progress with the source of our anxiety, for instance if our relationships or experiences regularly provoke anxiety, we can feel the body sensations for weeks or even months, leading to bigger emotions, such as panic.

Anger and frustration are often accompanied by a red face, headaches, shoulder tension, and sweat. They can cloud our thinking, driving us to combust and yell something we later regret. Patience evaporates along with any ability to analyze and work out problems. And forget empathy. It's really hard to muster any understanding for what it must be like in someone else's shoes if we are burning up inside.

Sadness can show up as a lump in our throat, low energy, depression, negative self-talk, and, of course, tears. We might notice our heart actually hurts when the sadness is due to relationship conflict—when someone important to us is not available, unresponsive, or won't talk, and we don't know why.

Fear reveals itself as racing or foggy thoughts as we catalogue all the reasons why something won't work out. It can also present as energy bursts that make concentration difficult, or impatience that manifests as a physical moving away or abruptly stopping a conversation. It can appear as indigestion, constipation, emotional eating, or chronic abdominal discomfort. Fear can prompt feelings of failure that can last for weeks, landing us in a rut of negative thinking and prompting us to make choices in our life and relationships that only exacerbate our fears. It can also freeze our ability to make decisions. For example, we try so hard to be a

Our Most Common Fears

- Fear of failure
- Fear of doing it wrong
- Fear of people not liking us
- Fear of the unknown
- Fear for our tween's safety
- Fear of the future
- Fear that people will leave us

good parent, a good partner, and to be good at the things we take on. Still, fear can utterly block our way. It's kind of like the devil we dance with is better than the one standing unknown on the sidelines. So we stick with what is familiar, even if it is harmful.

3. Consider your thoughts.

Once we've named what we are feeling, we must sift through the many voices in our head (yes, we all have them) and register the thoughts that come with our emotions, because it is our thoughts that can ultimately lead us to damaging, unhealthy behaviors in our relationships and the regret or guilt we may later feel about our actions. Or not. For example, in an argument with our tween, the internal messaging can range from *I am failing as a mother again, I will never be good at this* and *There is something wrong with this family; I cannot stop it* to *I feel taken advantage of, My kid is rude*, and more. In nearly every instance, these types of thoughts have no bearing on a productive way forward in the moment. But we cannot dismiss them and find a better approach without first acknowledging them. In the same situation, we might also think, more productively, *My kid has been struggling all week. She has something to say, and she really has not been able to communicate about it. I can help her out with this by sitting with her and listening. That will go a long way even if I don't feel like we fixed it.* If this is not where we start with our thoughts, we can end up here.

The Power of the Pie Graph

There are a lot of moving parts when we talk about our feelings—where they stem from and how we think and act based on them. It is hard to notice in the moment what is happening. You may be able to recognize when you need to slow down. But then what? One of the tools I use with clients to help them understand their thoughts and what is *really* driving their behavior is the pie graph.

We use a pie graph to assign different weights to the various reasons behind our feelings. It helps us translate our thoughts, put them in perspective, and ultimately alter a destructive conversational course with our tween. We can use it to dig deep into ourselves to grasp what we are experiencing and the emotions the experience is triggering, as well as regain control of our actions. It also gives us a way to spot a soil issue *in the moment of frustration* when it is rearing its insidious head, or to recognize that the disconnection we are experiencing with our tween in fact has nothing at all to do with a soil issue. Rather, it could be a *pattern of interaction* with our tween that is working our last nerve, and nothing more. (Often, it is a combination of both.)

Pie Graph 101

There are several ways to use a pie graph. The first is straightforward and works like this:

- Your tween calls you out for being late to pick them up. You're mad they have the audacity to say you're late (five minutes is not late), and you do so much for your child! You feel your blood pressure rise, your cheeks turn red. *If my tardiness is a problem, you can just walk!* you think.
- Another part of you may feel a bit embarrassed, because in truth, you see most of the other kids have been picked up and a child should not have to call out a parent for a life skill like this.
- Still another part of you may feel inadequate because you know you are often late, and though you are trying to do better, here is proof that you are still missing the mark.
- And then there is the part of you that hates being late and swore you never would be, because your parents were always late and you remember how much you despised that, so you feel a bit of sadness as well that you let down your tween.

Your pie graph might look like this: 40 percent assigned to anger, 20 percent assigned to embarrassment, 20 percent assigned to feeling inadequate, and 20 percent is sadness.

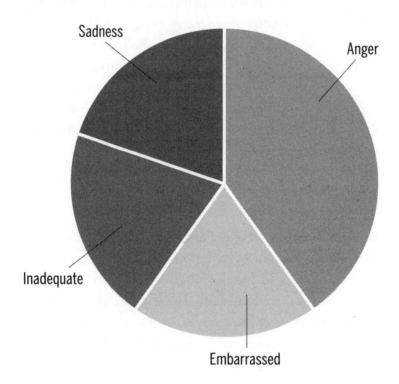

These percentages are personal and more for you to assess what you're experiencing. There is no right or wrong…or shame. In this example, anger is the biggest slice, because it is the adrenaline the parent is feeling that is driving their behavior (yelling, blaming the tween for how they responded to being late). Of course when we unpack it a bit more, we can see the other feelings that are fueling the anger.

When we tease out what we're feeling and why, we can isolate the part that is important to our relationship with our tween and discuss it with them. We can own our lateness saying something like, "I do see I'm five minutes late and other kids have been picked up. I know that makes you anxious. If you can give me a five-minute window, I will make a conscious effort to always be within it for picking you up. You are important to me and I know this is important to you."

We can also see the part that is about the kid in us who was left and how it made us feel anxious and unimportant. Recalling this and acknowledging it in the moment it appears equals awareness of a soil issue and the first step toward mastering it. The soil issue reminds us of what we don't want. Calling on our perspective, we can then see this for the unpleasant memory that it is, telling ourselves it need not happen now. We are an adult now with control over our life and choices, including, in this instance, making a conscious decision to be on time. There is such comfort in this, such relief.

Pie Graph Yin and Yang

The second way we use a pie graph is to map positive and hard feelings that occur simultaneously. It's a bit more complex. Here's an example.

- Your tween gets into an argument with another kid at school and says some mean things. The child's parent calls you to share their disappointment in your child. You talk with your tween and realize she was sticking up for a girl who was being left out by a small group of girls, including the daughter of the mom who called. (For the record, often we miss the backstory. We focus on the call, what was said, and never get to the motive behind our tween's actions.)
- Part of you is embarrassed that another parent saw your daughter in a "mean" light and worries that mom will tell other moms. Then there is a part of you that is offended your daughter said mean things and couldn't find another way to communicate. But there is a larger portion of you that is so proud she stood up for someone being mistreated.

Your pie graph might look like this: 15 percent assigned to "worried what the mother who called thinks about my daughter and who she will tell"; 10 percent to offended; and 10 percent to "embarrassed my daughter would talk to someone that way"; and 65 percent to "proud my daughter stuck up for somebody being left out."

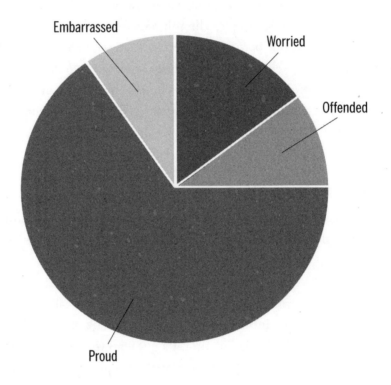

Because you asked for your tween's side of the story and took the time to understand her point of view, you could map out and understand your contradictory feelings then empathize with your daughter's tough position, praise her for standing up for her peer, and maybe talk about some alternative language she might have used. Plainly, if we are driven by worry and embarrassment, our reaction will be different than if we are driven by curiosity and pride.

The Mother of All Pie Graphs

When our feelings and our reactions are much bigger than a situation warrants, we can be certain something else is going on. Our pie graph can help us discover what it is. With this type of pie graph, instead of focusing on our different feelings, we look at *where* our feelings are coming from.

- How much of what we are experiencing is about the current interaction?
- How much is due to a maddening pattern we may be caught in with our tween?
- How much of our reaction is based on another difficult situation that is being triggered?
- How much of our reaction is based on a family-of-origin experience?

Here's how this pie graph works: I see my son in the same shirt he had on yesterday, the one he slept in last night. I ask, "Why are you wearing that shirt again?!" Not *Good morning.* Not *How did you sleep?* Not *So for breakfast we have x, y, and z. What would you like?* My tone is sharp, my eyes are piercing, and my mouth is tight. He picks up on it immediately and hisses back something about wanting to go back to bed. Mentally, I conjure my pie graph and use it to slow down, take a breath, and examine why I was so quick to respond in such a strong way. Here's what I discover:

- I'm irritated he thinks it is okay to wear the same clothes to bed and then to school. I think to myself, *just make good choices.* If I was just parenting from this feeling, my reaction could have been matter-of-fact: I could have simply told him that wearing the same clothes to bed and school the next day isn't a long-term habit he wants to develop. But there is so much more going on for me than the current situation.

- I'm irritated and downright angry he's wearing the same shirt. I want him in clean clothes, and he should value that. He is old enough, and we have discussed this ad nauseum. This isn't a new conversation between us; it is our pattern. I tell him something important (i.e. wear clean clothes) and he dismisses me. And it's not just about clothes; it's about his room, brushing his teeth, etc.

- But there is something else here for me, something that makes my reaction bigger than it needs to be and harder to recover from. I sit in irritation and anger and can't get over it before he leaves for school. I dig deeper and find the part of me that worries kids will start to notice and make fun of him. He will feel embarrassed and want to withdraw from school. I remember what it was like to feel my peers tease me; it was embarrassing. I would like to help him avoid feeling what I did. So my previous difficult situations with peers impact my feelings and how I express them, even before I consciously recognize it.

- Still, I know there's more. My reaction was just too strong. I dig again and find a soil issue from my family of origin. I'm afraid. If I cannot control him, if I cannot make him "good," I fear he will fail in life. It is the worst-case scenario, but I know it could happen based on my past experiences in my family.

My pie graph looks like this: 50 percent of my reaction was based on my family-of-origin fear that he would fail in life. It was the biggest driver behind my intense reaction. Our pattern of telling him something and feeling dismissed also played a large role in my feelings and reaction, maybe 30 percent. And probably 10 percent of my reaction was based on knowing how peers can be mean; I didn't have a lot of that teasing but I certainly saw other kids get teased ruthlessly, so I know how much it can hurt. And the irony of it all is this particular situation was only about 10 percent of my feelings and reactions. Do I really care if he wears clean clothes he wore to bed if they are weather appropriate, had not been played in, and don't look dirty or wrinkled? Not really.

When I am aware of what is driving my reaction, I can be more intentional about how I communicate. In this case with my son, I realized the irrational fear from my soil issue caused me to bark at him. When he came home from school, we were able to have a reasonable conversation. I owned my overreaction then re-emphasized why hygiene and habits matter.

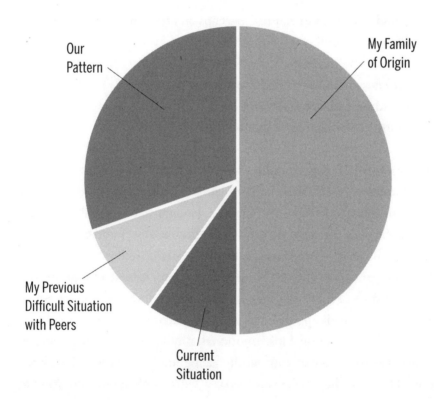

4. Connect the dots.

So now we've noted our physical reaction and matched it to a feeling and thoughts. The pie graph may be helping us begin to understand how to link current and past experiences. This is a key next step in developing the self-awareness we need to remediate our soil. When our behavior is instinctive and distances us from our tween, or we feel guilty later about an interaction with them, we have likely run head-on into a soil issue. If this happens to you, see if you can come up with other times in your life where you have experienced similar physical reactions, feelings, thoughts, and behaviors. Chances are, you will uncover some unhealed part of yourself that reveals itself with certain triggers. Which of the scenarios we described in the previous chapter might be the culprit?

- Childhood pain or trauma, perhaps an attachment injury?
- Partner discord?
- Day-to-day distress?
- Developmental stage disconnect?
- Children with special needs?
- Untreated addiction or mental illness?

To gain a better understanding of yourself, you may want to look at old photo albums or talk with family members about your childhood and see what emerges. You might also create a genogram, or a family tree that includes behavioral patterns of specific family members and relationship closeness or distance between the family members.

For your genogram, include yourself, your parents, and your grandparents on both sides of the family. For each person, add what you know about hurts, traumas, and disappointments such as alcohol or substance abuse, divorce, conflicted relationships, emotional, physical, and/or sexual abuse, etc. Once you have created your family genogram, step back and look for patterns. How did they make you feel as a kid? Think about how you are impacted by your family patterns today. Do any persist? Which ones have you triumphed over? Which ones haunt you?

Here's a sample of just one genogram. There are as many variations on genograms as there are families in the world.

You can also create a timeline charting the highs and low of your life. Include special family events such as graduations, births and deaths,

Sample Genogram

illnesses, marriages, moves, jobs, relationships, successes, failures, social and cultural themes, strengths, or special talents and rituals—anything that stands out in your life. Literally draw a straight line and plot each item based on how it impacted your life. It should surface the most important stories in your life, though you can use the timeline to zero in on a specific trigger as well. People usually identify with one of four core painful feelings from childhood such as shame, failure, rejection, or abandonment. Examine the feelings you find and the stories behind them.

Once you have a visual sense of your life and the stories most meaningful to you through the genogram or timeline, see if you can link childhood experiences to the way you respond to your tween in various situations. Be prepared to name any patterns you find, understand them, and appreciate (with self-compassion) that these are your soil issues. When we link today's frustrations toward our tween to our soil issues, we can start to see what is triggered by family-of-origin patterns or past traumas and what reactions and feelings are about right now with our tween. For instance, when my tween skips lunch and grabs a bunch of sugar twenty minutes later and I yell at him, I wonder if there is deeper meaning to my anger. I'm angrier than I should be for this situation. It could be we did not have a lot of money for food growing up and did not waste anything. Or it could be we didn't have nutritious options or a parent actually making meals, so I am angry at his lack of appreciation for my efforts. If I see him reaching for the sugar and I stay regulated and mildly irritated, I can see within myself that I am disappointed by his choices and can parent his poor choices as my adult self, not from my soil issues. Here's how my timeline for this scenario might look.

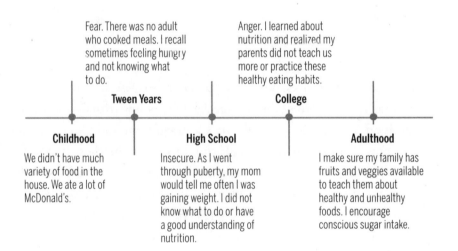

Sample Timeline

Fear. There was no adult who cooked meals. I recall sometimes feeling hungry and not knowing what to do.

Anger. I learned about nutrition and realized my parents did not teach us more or practice these healthy eating habits.

Tween Years

College

Childhood

We didn't have much variety of food in the house. We ate a lot of McDonald's.

High School

Insecure. As I went through puberty, my mom would tell me often I was gaining weight. I did not know what to do or have a good understanding of nutrition.

Adulthood

I make sure my family has fruits and veggies available to teach them about healthy and unhealthy foods. I encourage conscious sugar intake.

5. Manage emotions: The Emotion Scale.

We can give ourselves the best chance to succeed in the moment with our tween by keeping a sharp eye on the intensity of our emotions and managing them intentionally. One of the most effective ways for doing this is the Emotion Scale. It's a tool I use with tweens and adults in my practice, and it works like this:

It's based on a range of 1 to 10:

- 1 to 3 are mild emotions. We may feel irritated, but things are in control. We are still able to tolerate our tween's emotions, to talk and listen. We are open to different points of view. We are regulated in mind and body. We have enough emotion and stress to feel alive and motivated but not so much that it is affecting us negatively. We feel good, strong, and optimistic. We have energy to set boundaries. Our tween is calm, silly, childlike, open. We are able to walk away and concentrate on other tasks or people rather than get stuck in any frustration we may feel.

- 4 to 6 are medium emotions; they distract us, taking our thoughts from what we are doing to the people and places that bother us, but they haven't taken over…yet. It's the slippery slope. I call this the bridge. It's the beginning of dysregulation and the point at which we can catch ourselves and return to the calm of 1 to 3, or let fly. This is the time for intervention—anything that calms our emotions and positions us better to respond to others and tolerate their heavy emotions. The bridge is also the place to determine if there is a link between what we're feeling and a soil issue.

- 7 to 9 are the really intense emotions; they take over, completely blocking our ability to concentrate or act intentionally. Our nervous system is throbbing and we are dysregulated. Once we feel an emotion at a 7, it is hard to rein it in. It's like sliding on ice. There's a chance we'll catch ourselves, but it will be difficult. Our brain has initiated its stress response; adrenaline is flooding our body. This is the time we need to step away. Nothing good comes of conversations at this point. We must accept the slide through the top of the scale and wait for our emotion to run its course before we can return to a regulated baseline. We must also give our tween space if they get to 7, 8, or 9: They cannot talk it through with us or hear our reasoning when their emotions are running this hot.

- 10 is extreme and comes with rage. We lose our sense of now. Life may feel surreal. We may plummet into panic attacks, tics, and seizures, etc. It is complete dysregulation. For our tween, a 10 may present with tantrums or talk of self-harm.

Now consider our reaction in a given situation: The 1 to 3 range is like a check-engine light. It gives us the chance to catch ourselves, notice what is happening in our body, attach a feeling to it, associate it with its root cause and diffuse the emotion. This is ideal. We have the most clarity when we see a situation unfolding.

As we practice weighing our emotions using this scale, we may identify a situation that has happened before with our tween and know what we're about to experience. Or we may recognize when our tween talks to us in a certain way it reminds us of a childhood experience that leaves us feeling unappreciated, misunderstood, and "in danger." When we slow down, we can use self-awareness to register what is happening in our body, name what we're feeling and thinking and why. We can assess whether or not our tween is triggering some pain from our childhood or just irritating us in the here and now. All this helps us stay in the 1 to 3 range and make better choices in how we respond. It gives us the mental room to recognize that while our tween may be naughty, impulsive, and, at times, rude, they are *not* dangerous to our safety or self-worth. We are then able to consider what is *really* going on with our tween when they speak disrespectfully rather than viewing it as a reflection of ourselves. Perhaps they are hungry or struggling with some other situation and taking it out on us. In the 1 to 3 range, we can ask questions to find out. We can empathize.

For example, my son kept coming back to me to ask for a cell phone. Each time he asked, it was like we'd never discussed it before. Rather than caving to impatience, I thought *Oh my, we are on the cell phone again. I guess I'm not surprised he keeps talking about it. Apparently he thinks everyone else in his entire school except him has one. I imagine he feels left out.* My empathy kept me in the 1 to 3 range and gave me a place to join him in discussing this.

When we hit the 4 to 6 bridge on the Emotion Scale, we dysregulate. We either cross that bridge into actions we may later regret (anger, withdrawal) or examine what is happening within us and bring ourselves back to regulation.

For example, using a variation on the cell phone scenario, perhaps we're minding our own business when our tween enters the room and launches in on wanting a cell phone. Although we have had this conversation countless times before, our tween—like my son—asks as if it is the first time we are discussing this. Initially, we answer their questions (again). But as they persist, we can feel our temperature rising, adrenaline and anger start to flood our body. We snap: "We've talked about this already, a ton! You are not getting a phone so stop asking!" We are on the bridge; we are either going to calm ourselves back to the 1 to 3 range or explode to 7 and beyond with something like, *You're so ungrateful and think everything should just be handed to you. What is wrong with you? You're so entitled. Keep asking and I may never get you a phone!*

Yes it's annoying our tween is begging for a phone and, yes, as they get irritated it is normal for us to become more frustrated and go from a 2 to a 4 on the Emotion Scale. But when we cross the bridge to 7, 8, and 9, something else is happening in us. Maybe the relationship with our tween has gotten to the point with all their badgering that we feel in a constant state of being taken advantage of. Perhaps this has conditioned our system to go on a tense high alert even before they start talking and we get frustrated faster: The relationship itself is causing the disconnect we feel with our tween. Or maybe we did not have a lot as a kid, and to hear our tween demand something expensive surfaces feelings of not being good enough, reminding us of the sacrifices we made or the fact that our tween doesn't understand that part of us. Perhaps we feel unappreciated and angry at our child's sense of privilege in the face of how we grew up. Note: Feelings of failure, being taken advantage of, and shame are often at the top of the list when our reaction is bigger than a situation warrants.

At 7 to 10 on the Emotion Scale, we are fully dysregulated. Our tween's behavior has triggered a deeply engrained soil issue. We are most likely not even aware it has happened. For example, our unconscious brain may recall a time when we felt alone and misunderstood, judged, or criticized as a child; these feelings surface when our tween starts yelling that we don't get them. Shame runs through our body. To escape it, we fight. Again, this is all happening subconsciously.

The Emotion Scale

Range	What We Feel	The Actions We Take
1 to 3	Mild annoyance, motivated, regulated	Listen to our tween, imagine what they experienced, ask questions, pace the conversation to maintain calm, validate our tween's experience.
4 to 6 (The Bridge)	Temperature rising, patience wears thin	Pie graph our reaction to identify what we're feeling; tease out our tween's issue and how it might be affecting their behavior; take a break to catch our breath.
7 to 9	We are dysregulated, our tween is dysregulated: The wheels are off and nothing we do or say will end well	Ask for space and return later to pick up the conversation, and when we do, own our part for what we contributed to the pyrotechnics and start again with curious questions.
10	Rage	If you or your tween are in danger of self-harm, suicide, or homicide, you *must* seek outside help. Plainly. Still, I know it can be hard to ask but these typically are not isolated incidents. Over time they become scarier.

When we launch from these feelings and thoughts, we yell, threaten, name call, blame, attack, or withdraw by walking away or refusing to interact. (We hurt our tween as much with our silence as we do with our shouting.) In fact, all of these fight-or-flight reactions are our brain working to keep us safe, based on stored knowledge reactivated by our interaction with our tween. It registers our tween as dangerous as the interaction triggers hurtful past experiences. Oddly, when we come out swinging for our own safety we scare our tween. They look around wondering where the danger is, not realizing you are experiencing *them* as the threat. Instead, they feel the danger as well and react accordingly toward us.

It's a wicked spiral, and it happens to all of us. (Remember the beginning of chapter 11? We must always extend compassion to ourselves.) And when it does, we must remember we can make amends, take responsibility, let our tween know the interaction felt bad for us, and apologize with phrases such as *I did not understand what you were saying, I know that hurt your feelings*, or *I lost my temper and I know that is scary for you to experience*. This honesty and humility can defuse volatile situations and reopen a dialogue with our tween.

When tweens know what we are thinking and trust us to understand when their feelings are hurt, they open up and share their thoughts or fears. It may take more than once to repair our relationship when we tip into the higher end of the Emotion Scale, but every step forward is a plus for both of us.

CHAPTER THIRTEEN

SELF-SOOTHING AS WE NAVIGATE OUR SOIL ISSUES

As we work to recognize and remediate our soil with self-compassion and self-awareness and make the changes that will lead us to emotional connection with our tween, there are a range of self-soothing strategies to help us tolerate our emotions and bring us back to a regulated place of calm along the way.

Caring for Our Inner Child

Self-soothing techniques help us no matter where we may find ourselves on the Emotion Scale, except at the upper reaches, where they may be hard to access in the moment. Certainly self-soothing crosses streams with self-awareness: naming the dilemma in which we may find ourselves; recognizing that our tween's behavior may be awakening negative emotional memories from our childhood; activating a damaging voice from our "inner child." To counter this, as nutty as it sounds, I often counsel my clients to speak to that long-ago inner child…because it works. I ask them to find an image of their inner child: What age is the child? What does he or she look like? What is he or she doing? This gives people a visual of who they are dealing with. It's kind of like looking under the bed as a kid and realizing there isn't a large, scary monster there. It's the same with our inner child: When we visualize the child, we see it is an abstract neurological reaction, not a person ready to hurt us.

Next, we talk about language to share with the inner child to let him or her know they are safe, that this is not a repeat experience, and the adult within them can and will take care of the situation. This actually calms the brain, returning us to a regulated place from which we can interact more productively with our tween—to set boundaries, for instance, for their safety and education, rather than as an angry response to their behavior. It may be slow going at first, and we may have to take a moment away from our tween to do it. But, as we practice, it will come more quickly. Our inner voice of shame, failure, or abandonment will push back and want to remind us of all the reasons we are actually "in danger" or "not good enough." But we can fight back! We are in charge, not some inner child who doesn't have the slightest clue about what it is to be a wife, mom, husband, father, friend…adult.

The Two-Jar Jam

I use this a lot with the tweens I counsel and their parents. It is an essential soothing strategy because it helps parents find their calm to maintain emotional connection with their tween when emotions are firing in all directions. It works like this: Picture two jars, one in each hand. One holds *our* feelings and frustrations, *our* beliefs about how something should be, and *our* convictions for what should be done next in a situation unfolding with our tween. The other holds what *our tween* is experiencing. We can see what's inside each jar, but even when full, or worse, overflowing, we can still avoid a catastrophic spill of splattering mess and stains on our relationship with our tween by maintaining our hold.

When my jar overflows, I can let it go, for example by walking away or battling to be understood. *Or* I can hold on to it. When we hold both jars, we are able to placate our pain *and* get to the bottom of what's really going on with our tween. It's how we're still able to see our tween when we are losing it. We have the empathy to hear their perspective on a story, see their hurts, and know when they are flooded. This lets our tween know they can count on us to be calm and responsive to their needs: We *will* listen, we *will* spend quality time with them.

To recognize and understand ourselves and our tween (or anyone, for that matter), we have to be able to hold two different realities at once. If we overidentify with our own experiences and become so tied to our feelings and beliefs in a given situation, we will be unable to empathize. It's how we can get so off track and unable to see our tween's point of view.

When our jar overflows and we can't maintain our hold, our vision narrows. We can no longer see our tween. This is the time to step back, soothe our inner child, note our body sensations, our thinking, and link our current and past experiences until we can once again hold our feelings about an experience in our jar and also see what our tween's jar holds.

The Calm of Empathy

One of the best ways to soothe ourselves is by extending empathy. It is impossible to be angry and compassionate at the same time. To activate empathy on command, we must know what we feel in our body when we are empathetic. We can watch for the beating of our heart, the smile on our face, the calm we feel. These bodily sensations activate the part of our brain that feels sympathy and closeness to others. They will happen when we are in harmony with our children and last only a few seconds at first, but over time, we can stretch these moments. With practice, we can find empathy even when we are upset with our tween or they are angry at us, *if* we remember not to take their behavior personally.

We know our tween does not yet have anywhere near our experience, perspective, or neurological resources (which we learned in Part Two: It's Not You, It's Neuroscience). We can use this knowledge to find empathy, and rather than matching aggravation for aggravation, we factor in their developmental stage, recognizing they are struggling and need support and encouragement. When we stop and take a moment to listen to their pain as pain, see their hyperness as restlessness, realize they are telling the same story again and notice their voice is so loud, we can see them in their struggle. We can start to imagine what it's like to be in their shoes. When we focus on *their* experience, we are less focused on *our* experience. Their discomfort is real to them. As we empathize, we ignite an oxytocin release, the bonding hormone we talked about at the beginning of Part Three: What Lies Beneath.

Cultivate Connection

Oxytocin soothes our fight-or-flight response. When we are patient with our tween and open and curious about them, we feel connected, warm. We can cultivate the release of oxytocin through them in ways big and small. For example, in addition to empathizing, we can intentionally set aside five minutes to speak with them in the morning, after school, before bed (you'll find the five minutes go fast, and you stay longer the more often you do this); we can let them lead dinner conversation or share their favorite thing—even if we find it annoying. It can happen as we watch them, sit with them, focusing on the parts of them that are interesting, funny, and excited, and as we see this emerging person, once a helpless baby in our arms and now starting to find their way around the bigger world. Note: In contrast, when we are on the defense with our tween, we suppress the release of oxytocin, which impacts our ability to reach for our children and keeps us higher on the Emotion Scale (e.g., 7 and up, "over the bridge").

Ode to Joy

Joy is a quintessential self-soother as well, and we can train our brain to generate it on demand in our parenting. When we feel the rewards of parenting—the closeness, the love, the delight—we release dopamine, that happy hormone we also discussed in Part Three. We can activate a dopamine release by observing and delighting in our tween—catching their growing wisdom, wit, and smarts; looking at pictures of them; listening to their voice around the house or with friends; hearing their excitement about something; focusing on their tone as they talk with us; being open about how they feel and use their assertiveness to share their desires. Doing this regularly also helps us develop more tolerance of our tween's emotional changes. Once we get in a habit of activating dopamine, our brain will store these memories and the rewarding experiences that come with them, making it easier to stay calm when we're on that bridge of the Emotion Scale.

CHAPTER FOURTEEN

WORK IN PROGRESS

It is important to remember no one changes overnight. The first opportunity to modify our behavior, and every chance thereafter, will most likely be no Hollywood moment. (And anyway, remember: Perfection is *not* our goal.) Rather, we manage our expectations and celebrate the progress as we move through the change. It goes like this:

1. **Recognize there is a behavior that needs changing.** Be clear about what isn't working and what we want to change. For instance, let's say we don't want to criticize or yell at our tween. Then, we recognize what is occurring in our body, and the thoughts and feelings that accompany our behavior, so that we are ready to preempt it as soon as it begins to emerge. We can pie graph the moments to see what is leading to our behavior. Is there a soil issue involved?

2. **Develop alternative ways we would like to respond in those moments.** A plan gives us a vision and direction, a road map to fall back on when we dysregulate or are caught off guard. But remember, implementing it will be a journey; It will not happen instantly.

3. Once we have our target behavior and our plan, we can **understand that next time the response is triggered, we will likely exhibit the same behavior** (yelling or criticizing) and then realize after the fact we did it again. This is because we are still developing our

ability to achieve in-the-moment awareness. Nevertheless, spotting the behavior, even after the fact, is progress. We caught it, we realized it wasn't helpful, we felt its negative impact on us (guilt, disappointment); we saw it on our tween's face, and we now have the opportunity to own our part, which will strengthen our awareness for the next time. We also have the chance to repair what just happened with our tween by saying something like, *Hey I want you to know I recognized when I said that earlier in frustration it didn't feel good to you and I am sorry, I certainly don't want to hurt your feelings.*

4. **At some point, we may realize in the moment that we are repeating a mistake, stop and try a different behavior.** Often the new behavior isn't the ideal change we are striving for: We are, after all, practicing something new. At this stage, tweens report their parents are insincere or awkward. Parents will say it doesn't feel genuine or they are letting their tween win. We have to fight through it. This unsettling and frustrating time is about changing and practicing new behaviors until we find something that fits for us and our tween. It is a necessary part of the process, and each step, no matter how small, is progress!

5. **And then we will triumph!** A time *will* come when we see our old behavior pushing to come through in the moment. As if in slow motion, we feel ourselves heating up, defaulting to the behavior we're trying to change. The pull will be strong, but we slow down enough to catch it early, hold our emotion in the jar, and try a new behavior that connects with our tween. We might create some room to settle ourselves by saying something like *Excuse me for a moment, I feel myself getting frustrated and don't want to yell so let's slow this down.* Or, we might ask, *Can you say that a different way because I really want to hear what you're saying?* We will find our new behavior works; the connection with our tween will remain intact even during a conflict. We will feel the victory!

Inevitably, we will slip back to old behaviors even after our wins. Everyone does. But with self-compassion, self-awareness, and intentionality, we can create the foundation needed to build the kind of emotional connection with our tween that will last a lifetime. We will also feel stronger and healthier mentally, more confident about our parenting strategies, and that will trickle into other areas and relationships in our life.

Faith gives us the confidence to understand and accept ourselves with all our imperfections. After all, God does. It reminds us that we are each unique, with our own God-given gifts to share with the world, that forgiveness (especially self-forgiveness) and fresh starts are universal, that we are not alone in this: There is help on this journey if we are willing to help ourselves. It gives us the lift we need to take the leap: to care, love, fight, stretch, create boundaries, and launch into our life in a meaningful way. If we pay attention, there are plenty of signs, those "winks from God" I spoke of earlier that tell us we are on the right path. (Any misery we might continue to feel tells us we most certainly are not!)

QUESTIONS TO PONDER

1. Imagine your inner child—source of that critical inner voice that drives you toward dead ends. Can you hear yourself tell him or her they are *not* driving; they *are* safe so there is no need for any commentary from them?

2. What words do you use to offer yourself the kindness and grace to be you? Can you make a declaration to allow and even invite self-compassion? A declaration is several sentences to a paragraph or two detailing how and why you show kindness and care toward yourself. You may list your support systems and why you count on them. Think of people you know who are nurturing, wise, and protective, someone you can lean on when you are struggling.

3. Using the Emotion Scale, what can you do to feel better when your emotions are a 1 to 3, 4 to 6, and then 7 to 10?

4. Which of the self-soothing strategies described in this chapter fits best for you?

PART FIVE

Dancing Neurons

Feedback Loops:
The Patterns We Create

"When we embrace the possibilities the quantum worldview offers us, we invite defining moments—moments when we dare to venture into new terrain, transcending our struggles and actualizing new realities."

—MEL SCHWARTZ, MARRIAGE AND FAMILY THERAPIST, AUTHOR

"A gentle answer turns away wrath,
but a harsh word stirs up anger.
The tongue of the wise adorns knowledge,
but the mouth of the fool gushes folly."

—PROVERBS 15:1 NIV

When I discovered feedback loops, I thought I was learning magic. When I started uncovering the patterns of interactions between family members that comprise feedback loops, I *knew* I had found magic, a way to make sure the relationship seeds we plant land on "good soil." Feedback loops show us how our feelings drive our behavior toward one another. We can actually *see* them in action if we know what to look for.

So far, we've learned about the key to our relationship with our tween: emotional connection. We've examined the tween brain and the fascinating yet non-negotiable neurological shifts occurring in their head space. We've looked at how our own childhood experiences, family-of-origin connections, and attachment style are baked into our past and impact how we parent and instinctually handle emotional connection. We've also learned how to remediate the soil issues that may be hurting our relationship with our tween.

We've arrived at a tipping point: We've gotten through the hardest part of the book…hard because self-examination can be rough, and we cannot change the past. We also cannot change what's happening in our tween's brain or the facts of emotional connection. But we *can* change our feedback loops to build emotional connection. Feedback loops can be strengthened, slowed down, redirected, or exchanged for a better version, as you will see from the information in this part.

So we're moving from what we can't change to what we can, using all that we've learned so far. In fact, we cannot move forward effectively to apply the tips and tools you will read about in the next section without what we've learned from the previous chapters. As you will see, it provides the context we need to succeed, informing our parenting decisions and actions, which become the relationship we have with our tween, the place where the seeds we plant can flourish.

I am truly blessed to have met and worked with thousands of families over the years. Most interesting to me has always been the pattern of interactions between family members. I often say the relationship between family members is my client. Because my goal is optimal health and wellness for the family system, I work with families to adjust their feedback loops. This is really cool stuff, so let's get to it.

CHAPTER FIFTEEN

ANATOMY OF A FEEDBACK LOOP

My style of therapy draws heavily from Emotionally Focused Therapy. Co-created by Sue Johnson, it is based in large part on feedback loops as a way we play out emotional connection (or the lack of it). Understanding and naming our feedback loops gives us a path to unlocking emotional connection with our tween, and all our family members, for that matter. It allows us to intervene when emotions are running hot and repair a relationship when it is injured.

What exactly are feedback loops? Fueled by emotion and expressed through behavior, feedback loops are the way we interact with each other, forming patterns that lead to our relationships. In these behaviors, a feedback loop is visible. It is a window into what we are feeling.

Feedback loops start with a behavior from one person that triggers an emotion in another. Think of how a lit match falls on a perfectly laid campfire—a couple pieces of fatwood, some newspaper, kindling, and twigs. Instantly, it catches, and you have a bonfire. Now think of that match as a behavior from our tween—igniting an emotion. Our brain absorbs their behavior, turns it into biochemical and electrical reactions, and activates neurons—specialized cells that transmit information throughout the body. An emotion is born. Our amygdala assesses the emotion to determine what's coming our way: Something we'll like? Something we won't? Is there danger—a disconnection from someone we love?

Emotions lead to behaviors such as a look from our tween, a nod of acceptance, a smile, a thank you, a hug, or a laugh if we are calm and happy; a scowl, a louder voice, intimidating posture, storming out of a room mid-conversation, and more if we are in the midst of conflict and hurt. Our tween's behavior will spark an emotion in us, which will lead to another behavior from our tween, which will trigger the next emotion and related behavior, and so on. A feedback loop is born.

For a parent (P), the pattern goes like this: Tween (T): behavior/trigger ➡ P: emotion ➡ P: behavior/trigger ➡ T: emotion ➡ T: behavior/trigger. It can also work the other way with the parent providing the initial trigger like this: Parent (P): behavior/trigger ➡ T: emotion ➡ T: behavior/trigger ➡ P: emotion ➡ P: behavior/trigger.

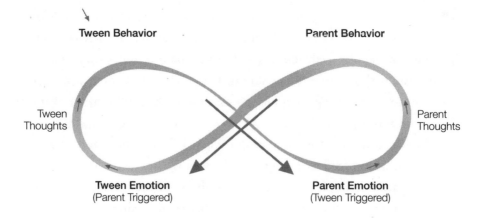

Now consider this: A human brain has nearly 100 billion brain cells. Brain cells fire roughly 200 times a second, sending neurochemical transmitters (messages) into the synaptic cleft—the space between neurons that helps nerve impulses pass from one to another.

Collectively this is called neuron activity, and it never stops, even when we are at rest or focused on just one task. It's always there in the background, driving our behavior. It's how our brain "feels" then translates those emotions into thoughts such as, *I feel hot, I feel cold, I am hungry, I like that girl, I feel important when my parents ask me about my day.*

The challenge is all that firing amounts to 11 million pieces of information per second, all of it stored in the brain for future reference. We consciously process just forty pieces of this information per second. While forty is better than 11 million for sure, it's still mind-boggling, literally. That's why we miss so much.

Feedback loops happen *fast*; they're automatic, and they are often impacted by previous interactions with our tween. Over time, what has come before becomes the working model of our unconscious reactions and how we feel about interactions with our family members, as we discussed in Part Three: What Lies Beneath.

Feedback loops are inevitable, an ongoing cycle, and a particular loop can persist for moments or days and weeks, as long as we keep triggering emotions in one another through our behaviors. We can have a variety of feedback loops with one family member (although usually one is dominant), and different feedback loops with other family members (and everyone we know, for that matter—but that's a topic for another book!).

Sometimes feedback loops are good and lead us to feel understood and closer to another person (emotionally connected). Sometimes feedback loops make us question ourselves and feel unsure, disconnected from people we love. In reality, we swing between good and bad feedback loops depending on what is being triggered in us.

Feedback loops are informed by our attachment style, because how we felt in a relationship with our parent(s) shapes the feelings that surface in our interactions with our tween. Feedback loops can also be influenced by experiences we had growing up—with students, peers, teachers, or other adults—our triumphs and our traumas, and our day-to-day challenges collectively, our soil issues. As you will see, feedback loops are also affected by previous patterns in our exchanges with our tween, as well as what is happening developmentally with their brain and other things that may be occurring in our life.

In other words, as we also discussed before, most of the relational messages our brain is processing are impacted by earlier interactions in our life and conditions we may not recall or even be aware exist. Conversely, our tween has virtually no wisdom and little relationship experience to draw from: Their reactions are based mostly on their low-functioning prefrontal cortex and overfunctioning amygdala you learned about in Part Two: It's Not You, It's Neuroscience, as well as the feedback loops they are accustomed to in their interactions with us. (If we are often in conflict with our tween or a particular topic inevitably sparks a disagreement, they approach our interactions defensively, suspicious of the argument they are conditioned to think will follow.) And of course, the attachment style to which we were exposed will be in our memory bank and used to interpret a behavioral interaction with them.

As you know from preceding chapters, while we can't do anything about where our tween's brain is—that's nature—or our past relationships, we *can* alter our feedback loops—that's nurture. Here's a look at one in action:

My client, I'll call her Amelia, hears her mom coming in the door from work and instantly feels a sense of frustration. She pivots from her homework to thinking about the discussion she wants to have with her; she wants Mom to change her mind about when and for how long she can use her phone. Her friends get as much phone time as they want until nine p.m. and then they are allowed to keep their phone in their room. Amelia can't use her phone after eight-thirty p.m. and is required to hand it over to her parents at that time. Amelia thinks she is missing out on her social life because of her parents' rules. She knows Mom is going to say no. She has said no to these requests before—a lot of times. As Amelia continues to think about her phone situation, her frustration intensifies. She can feel her heart beat faster.

Maybe Amelia would not feel so aggravated if she thought Mom was not going to say no *again*. Amelia's nervous system has her ready for a fight. Her amygdala is telling her danger is looming.

Amelia approaches Mom as she is going to the bathroom to change from her office clothes after a long commute home. "I think I should have more phone time and it's not fair," she says. Exhausted and still in office mode but determined to be consistent with limits and follow-through, Mom calmly explains why the rule is the rule and it is not going to change at this time. Amelia, fully prepped by her mindset, blows her top and yells at Mom about how unfair this is. Mom feels her own temperature rise, and her words become sharp and pressured. She is tough on Amelia, who sometimes feels so misunderstood and alone trying to fight for things that are important to her. But Mom never seems to care, always choosing the "right" answer without considering her feelings. She explains quickly and loudly why Amelia cannot have more phone time and threatens to take the phone away completely if she continues to complain. Amelia storms from the room, slamming the door as she leaves.

Here's a look at this feedback loop.

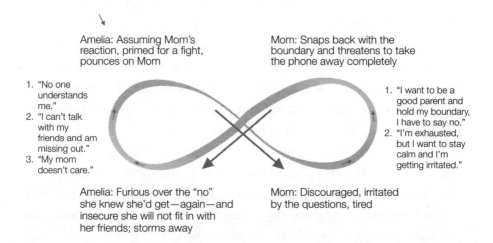

Amelia: Assuming Mom's reaction, primed for a fight, pounces on Mom

1. "No one understands me."
2. "I can't talk with my friends and am missing out."
3. "My mom doesn't care."

Amelia: Furious over the "no" she knew she'd get—again—and insecure she will not fit in with her friends; storms away

Mom: Snaps back with the boundary and threatens to take the phone away completely

1. "I want to be a good parent and hold my boundary, I have to say no."
2. "I'm exhausted, but I want to stay calm and I'm getting irritated."

Mom: Discouraged, irritated by the questions, tired

When you read this conversation between Amelia and her mother, did you think about the issue they are talking about (phone time) and try to solve it? Often, we listen to the words spoken to us and respond unconsciously to the *con*tent rather than the *in*tent. We don't think about how the interaction is emotionally impacting us or how our words might be impacting our tween, particularly given their hyper self-focus, social insecurity, and inability to project beyond the present moment. Rather, we follow what's ingrained. We cave to what comes naturally and miss the patterns. We don't see the feedback loops. It is the biggest problem we have with communication.

Now, go back and reread the exchange between Amelia and her mom. This time, look for the pattern they are using to communicate. Look at emotion and behavior separately for each of them. You will see this is not conversation. It's really two nervous systems reacting to each other. They both sent, received, experienced, and responded to messages sharing in a dance of language fueled by thought and emotion occurring in the brain and nervous system—a feedback loop.

Do you see how Amelia was ready for a fight even before her mom walked in the door, because all previous attempts to address something important to her gave her a response she didn't like, a threat to her agenda? Just thinking about it ramped up her nervous system, putting her one "no" away from popping off.

Amelia's mother, on the other hand, came in calm and confident, certain she was doing the right thing holding the line on the boundaries she and Amelia's dad had set. But her firm tone and strong boundary sent Amelia into orbit. Amelia's outburst threw Mom off as her nervous system picked up on the escalating conversation and prepared for a fight. In fact, she was unconsciously recalling her own past and thinking *Wait, setting this boundary makes me a good parent, right? It's supposed to keep Amelia from wasting time like I did so that she can do well in school. This is the best thing for her. Why then is she screaming at me? Am I not a good parent? How can this make me so distant from her?* Her calm morphed to discouragement and insecurity, prompting her to second-guess her decision, which escalated her response to a sharp tone and threats—emotion plus behavior—further enraging Amelia. And remember, most of those thoughts were occurring unconsciously for Amelia's mom.

While a difference of just thirty minutes between the phone time she has and what her friends are allowed may seem insignificant to us, for Amelia it's a disaster. Given where she is developmentally as a tween—hyper-aware of social norms and completely focused on self—a half hour may as well be ten hours, sparking thoughts such as: *If you have even two minutes more phone time than me, you're going to know I'm a loser. I'm being left out. I'm being left behind.* Tweens think *If I can't be the same as everyone else, people are going to think something is wrong with me.* These are emotional thoughts, and the tween brain does not yet have the capacity to recognize what's going on or explain it. It's just there so they respond irrationally. When parents can see this for what it is, we can react intentionally and reasonably rather than matching their emotional outburst with one of our own.

Here's what it could have looked like:

Amelia comes in primed for a confrontation. Mom does not take the bait. She stays neutral and lets Amelia know she can see something important is on her mind. Mom invites Amelia to sit down and discuss it. "I want to hear what you have to say. Just let me finish changing and we can talk."

Mom listens to Amelia's argument and asks her some questions so that she can be clear about what she is saying. "How late do you think you should have your phone?" and "Does that increase how long you are on your phone?"

Mom then shares what the phone rules currently are and why. When Amelia loses her top, Mom waits for her to talk. She paraphrases what she hears Amelia saying: "I see you're really upset that your phone time is not going to change. I also hear your friends have more lenient phone privileges." (Here Mom is empathizing, speaking to Amelia's disappointment—while she is aware her thoughts are starting to race as that old, frustrated feeling starts to drive her off an emotional cliff, she recognizes it and holds it so that she can meet Amelia where she is.)

Here's what this feedback loop looks like.

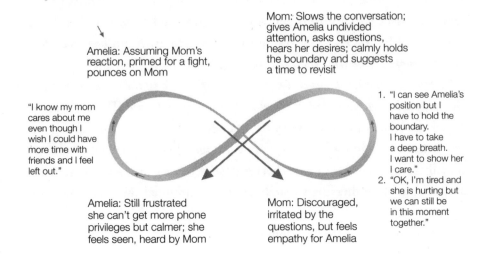

Mom: Slows the conversation; gives Amelia undivided attention, asks questions, hears her desires; calmly holds the boundary and suggests a time to revisit

Amelia: Assuming Mom's reaction, primed for a fight, pounces on Mom

"I know my mom cares about me even though I wish I could have more time with friends and I feel left out."

1. "I can see Amelia's position but I have to hold the boundary. I have to take a deep breath. I want to show her I care."
2. "OK, I'm tired and she is hurting but we can still be in this moment together."

Amelia: Still frustrated she can't get more phone privileges but calmer; she feels seen, heard by Mom

Mom: Discouraged, irritated by the questions, but feels empathy for Amelia

Faith can help us find the space needed to hold on to calm or stop a feedback loop midstream, to reverse course on a spiral that seems out of control. It gives us strength, direction, and peace, allowing us to shed our anger, our need to control and be right. It brings us back to the people we love. When we try our best to live with grace and gratitude, keeping our thoughts raised high and on people and things outside ourselves, we are better positioned to land in that open space between composure and wrath where there is still choice. We can elect to be aware of ourselves and our tween in the moment, to orchestrate an even exchange. We do this by paying attention to physical reactions—theirs and ours—facial expressions, body language, gestures, tone of voice, eye contact, and the pace we speak. When we are calm, our tone of voice is pleasant, the pace of the conversation is slower, we are listening to understand and empathize *not* to judge or correct. We want to let our tween know we hear them and understand what they are saying by listening, asking questions, and paraphrasing what we hear, maintaining eye contact. They will feel heard and understood. In being known, they will be calm, then we can offer our boundary. When our nervous system senses conflict or danger, we are more likely to raise our voice, blame, overexplain, talk fast, fidget, or storm away from a conversation. Usually, as you will recall from earlier in this chapter, this is because a strong emotion has been triggered by previous interactions with our tween or in other relationships. This is the difference between a positive and negative feedback loop. Watch for more on this in the Tools section, which comes next.

Positive Feedback Loops

When there is emotional connection, we feel a close relationship with our tween. Positive feedback loops are how we see emotional connection play out. When we are in a positive feedback loop with our tween, we are fully present in the moment. We are accessible, responsive, and emotionally engaged, available for conversation or play and not multitasking or on our way to the next thing.

In positive feedback loops, we are attuned to our tween. We've adjusted the dial and found their station. We listen, ask questions, comment, and work to understand what they're thinking and feeling, how they see things. We may not agree with them, and we may detect a lot of holes in their thinking, but we're showing them we want to understand their point of view. As a result, they feel safe, calm, comforted, heard, and supported because we are curious about them and express empathy for their situation.

We're telling them with our behavior that their opinions matter. Our tween feels valued. This builds their self-worth, and they will be more open to our take on a situation, hang longer with us, and share more. We can even set boundaries that are relevant to the conversation at hand.

In positive feedback loops, we are also co-regulating with our tween. In simple terms, this means we are mutually and unconsciously modifying our behavior based on what we each are doing. That is why a parent can walk in a room and say nothing, but their tween's demeanor will change. Or our tween walks in the room and says one word and we will either smile, happy to see them, or become guarded because our brain is preconditioned from past experiences to expect certain behaviors. It is why anxious parents so often have anxious children: They inadvertently transfer their worry to their child. On the other hand, a self-aware anxious parent can modify their behavior to achieve a different outcome, as my client does in the following situation:

A client, whom I will call Caleb in this scenario, and his mom sit down at the table with a snack after school. He is quiet and looks sad. Mom starts to ask him a ton of questions. She knows the look on his face. She has seen it before, often after a bad experience with his peers. She can feel her concern taking hold along with a desire to pressure him for answers. She desperately wants to comfort him. But she also knows from previous experience that if she comes in too hot, asking questions and presenting solutions, he will walk away.

Instead, she takes a deep breath, noticing her temperature rise as she backs off on the questions. She says a quick prayer for strength and keeps it easy, asking about his snack choice and what is next on his agenda. Then she asks about his day: "Was it a win, lose, or draw? What was the best thing, the worst thing, and something silly that happened?" Caleb doesn't respond. Instead of demanding an answer, Mom says simply: "Well, know I am here if you want to talk about your day." Caleb then proceeds to talk about other things, something he found interesting in his video game. He circles back to the silly thing that happened during the day then walks off. In truth, Mom is still worried, but she doesn't push. She decides to ask about his day again in a couple hours.

Because Caleb had a good experience with Mom just listening and not pushing, he feels more open to talk to her later. He winds up sharing what it was like to be in class and not understand what the teacher was talking about. Mom feels herself wanting to fix the problem. Her thoughts race: *Should I call the teacher? Do you want me to look over your homework with you? Should I call the special ed department again? Should we bring Dad into the conversation?*

But again, she knows from previous experience, going to this place makes Caleb freak out. Instead, she empathizes with him: "Wow, that stinks to be in class and see everyone else look like they understand the assignment and you don't. Did you feel left out?" Caleb answers: "Yes, I did. So I went to the bathroom, and when I came back, they were still working on the assignment, and now I am even more behind."

Mom again fights the temptation to talk fast about a solution, to tell him what he should do. Instead, she sits with him, takes a deep breath, and asks him what he did next. As he talks, she listens, maintaining eye contact and offering empathetic comments: "Ohh, that is the worst," and then, "What? Ugh. I know that feeling and it doesn't feel good, does it." What she *really* is saying is: *I care. I get you.* The more evenly she paces the conversation, slowly, intentionally, and calmly, the more Caleb shares. When he is finished talking, Mom asks: "What do you think you should do next?" Caleb comes up with a couple of options, and Mom invites him to pick one. She asks if it would be okay to check in tomorrow about it and he says, "Yes."

Here's their feedback loop.

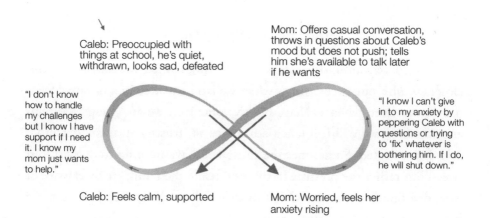

Caleb: Preoccupied with things at school, he's quiet, withdrawn, looks sad, defeated

Mom: Offers casual conversation, throws in questions about Caleb's mood but does not push; tells him she's available to talk later if he wants

"I don't know how to handle my challenges but I know I have support if I need it. I know my mom just wants to help."

"I know I can't give in to my anxiety by peppering Caleb with questions or trying to 'fix' whatever is bothering him. If I do, he will shut down."

Caleb: Feels calm, supported

Mom: Worried, feels her anxiety rising

The technique Caleb's mom used was like chasing a cat. If you run after it, you will never catch it. If you sit quietly and calmly, as if you don't see it, the cat will come around. If you remain calm, it will even sit with you. But any fast moves and the cat will run, just like a tween. Caleb's mom was emotionally impacted by what her son was saying and thinking. She was aware of her emotion and able to hold her natural instincts and instead attune with what Caleb was feeling. This allowed her to listen, imagine what his experience felt like, and access empathy for his situation.

Let me be clear: When we do this, we are not necessarily *agreeing* with our tween's opinions per se, but we are *understanding* what it is like from their perspective. Furthermore, it makes it easier for us to remain open to being wrong. In this case, Caleb's mom thought his sadness was a *peer* issue. She learns through listening that it was an *academic* issue. In addition, in remaining calm, especially after Caleb shared his classroom concerns, she modeled how to soothe her nervous system for her son.

This is about the time parents ask me what is in it for them. Up to now, we have met our tween, listened to them, let them act out their emotions. We have been patient, empathetic, and open. My answer is this: When we meet our tween's needs, they calm down and we calm down. Consequently, we are not in an intense emotional cycle of negative feedback loops: We are emotionally connected.

Negative Feedback Loops

There is no way around it: There will be times when we can't access this closeness with our tween, times when we land squarely in a negative feedback loop. Even when we have healthy practices, we are going to experience conflict, we will feel taken advantage of, frustrated, misunderstood, and disconnected. Sometimes the cause will have nothing to do with our tween but rather the pressure of things outside the family, such as work or extended-family soil issues. Other times it will be about their behavior and how it impacts our nervous system.

Tweens may push back on the boundaries we set. We may push them beyond their comfort zone or insist they do something they don't want to do to develop self-discipline. Or they may say things that trigger feelings of frustration in us. Other times our tween may be defiant, disrespectful, or too angry or irrational to empathize with. When these things happen, we often default to ingrained impulses and old patterns of behavior—a negative feedback loop.

In a negative feedback loop, the brain of both parent and tween automatically reacts in this way: The emotional processing center—the amygdala—interprets the information and sends a distress signal carried through a neuron to the hippocampus, the command center for emotions and motivation for the nervous system. It then dispatches a message, through another neuron, to the adrenal glands to pump the hormone epinephrine (adrenaline). Adrenaline prompts the release of glucose (sugar), which creates a burst of energy.

When this stuff comes on line, we can feel our body change—we get warm, our heart beats faster, and we breathe harder, which floods the brain with oxygen, enhancing our awareness of what is going on, then *BOOM!* Our neurons go wild, and we explode. Yell. Lose control. Say things we regret. Or we might walk away, leaving the conversation midstream. This is the stress response system kicking in (our sympathetic nervous system, as you will recall from Part One: Love Wins). We will fight, freeze, or flee. If the threat continues, our brain's command center sends messages to release cortical energy, which is what keeps us on alert. Co-regulation kicks in: We get revved up, our tween gets revved up, and vice versa. Remember, if this is happening to us as parents, the same body response occurs in our tween, compounded by their inability at this stage to understand, let alone articulate, what is going on.

At some point, the danger dissipates because emotion ebbs and flows, leaving guilt and frustration on both sides over unresolved issues, a bruised relationship, and a break in our emotional connection.

These interactions can become recurring, resulting in repeated arguments, punctuated by slammed doors or loud exclamations of disgust, or we ignore the issue and each other. Whether passive or active, each incident

STRESS RESPONSE

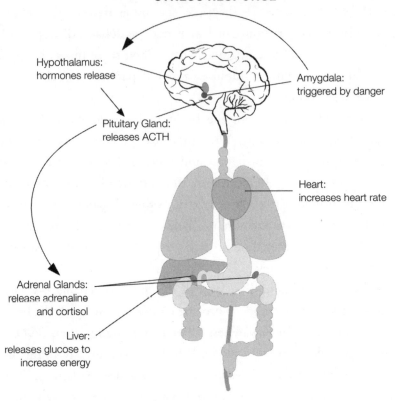

Hypothalamus:
hormones release

Amygdala:
triggered by danger

Pituitary Gland:
releases ACTH

Heart:
increases heart rate

Adrenal Glands:
release adrenaline
and cortisol

Liver:
releases glucose to
increase energy

reactivates our stress response. Over time, this takes a toll on our body and can lead to high blood pressure, artery-clogging deposits, trouble concentrating, anxiety, depression, and substance abuse. Because neither parent nor tween are happy, the feedback loop grows, and stress levels rise. Although we want to repair the connection, we go about it all wrong, doubling down on what's not working and feeding the conflict. Our tween winds up feeling misunderstood and ultimately unsafe.

We can get to a point where we feel as if we're sitting on a powder keg, just waiting for another explosion. Our emotional connection has been injured, the house is falling down! We feel disconnected, and tweens often say: "I can't talk to my mother about this," or "My father doesn't care what I do as long as I do my homework and get good grades." Parents respond: "My tween lies to me," or "If only they would do what they are supposed to do, we wouldn't have these problems," or "Why are they acting this way?"

Arguing between a parent and tween can cause marital conflict as parenting guilt, shame, or a sense of failure sets in, which complicates the relationship further. If these feelings are not acknowledged, the lack of self-awareness combines with emotional pain from a bruised tween relationship, and it will be difficult to parent effectively. Parents may shut down to protect themselves from future pain. Others may seek relief in alcohol or other addictions. In a family where there is little connection overall, loneliness, sadness, and loss can run rampant. Sibling relationships can suffer because of the discomfort and tension. Siblings can feel sad, pressured to walk on eggshells or be "the good kid." Collectively and not surprisingly, this does a number on a tween: It's not just the feedback loops between you and your tween impacting them but rather all the feedback loops within the family.

Let's take a look at a negative feedback loop:

Every time a client, whom I will call Kazdin, comes home from being with Mom, Dad says he seems mad. (Kazdin's parents are divorced. He lives with his dad and Mom shows up infrequently, at best.) No matter what Dad says or does, Kazdin returns looking for a fight, and he gets one. On this particular day, Kazdin comes in just before dinnertime. He is starving because he hasn't eaten since late morning. Kazdin had been on good behavior with Mom because he was so glad to see her and hoped if he was good she would come again soon. As it was, he had not seen her for two weeks before today.

Kazdin asks Dad when dinner will be ready. He says he hasn't started it yet, because he wasn't sure if Kazdin had eaten already. A seemingly mild comment from Dad sets Kazdin off. He blows up:

"How can you not have dinner ready? You don't care if I get fed or not. You always want me to take care of myself and you don't do anything for me!"

Although Dad is ready for some fight from Kazdin, the comments trigger his feelings of inadequacy as a parent. Dad worries about being a good parent and wants to get it right. Comments like this from Kazdin make him think that no matter how hard he tries, he is not being a good dad. He replies: "Watch your tongue, son. You can't talk to me that way. If it were up to your mom, you would never eat. So don't come in here talking to me about not being a good parent to you."

Dad's comments about his mom pierce Kazdin's heart, and he instantly feels sad knowing Mom isn't there for him when he needs her. But to be sad is not acceptable, because it implies weakness and might send him to a dark place he won't be able to get out of. So instead, he rages: "What the f$#)%*)($#*)! I don't want to eat with you," and storms off.

Here's a look at this feedback loop.

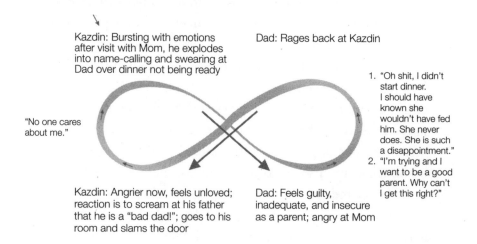

Kazdin was bursting with buried emotion before he even saw his mom. There have been so many times when she was late or canceled at the last minute that he worries for days leading up to her visits that she will not come. Then, while with her, he works hard to make the time fun. He is afraid if he shares his disappointment, she will be mad and not come back. So he holds in his frustration over her inconsistencies. It is an effort to be so good when they are together. He processes most of this unconsciously, unaware he's doing any of it. Not his nervous system, though: It knows exactly what's going on.

Dad assumes Kazdin goes through some difficult emotional stuff around his mom and feels responsible that he and Kazdin's mom aren't closer. He wishes he could make it all better. He feels he is not being a good parent and not doing enough for Kazdin. He feels guilty and insecure about this. It makes him tentative around Kazdin, which leads to defensiveness and yelling.

If we can see a feedback loop in process, slow down enough to recognize the emotions it is triggering (by pie graphing them, for example), and be more intentional in our behavior toward our tween, we can de-escalate the situation before it spins out of control and leaves us feeling guilty or angry. If we are unable to see what happened within our feedback loop until after a blowup, there is still an opportunity to repair the damage. We will talk about this next.

CHAPTER SIXTEEN

TURNING NEGATIVES TO POSITIVES: REPAIRING YOUR RELATIONSHIP

I s it easy to catch an emotion as it detonates, to calm ourselves and pivot to a different reaction? Absolutely not! We may notice the mistakes we're making in the moment, but we can't stop ourselves. Or, after the negative feedback loop has run its course, we may realize we could have handled it far more productively. That is why repair is so important. It starts with forgiveness, the kind we learn through faith to extend to others and ourselves. This helps us find the humility to admit our mistakes, apologize, and regain our footing. And when we show humility, own our part, and let our tween know we are sorry, we pave the way to repair.

Here's what happened with Kazdin and his dad.

Kazdin's dad takes time to reflect and forgive himself, which gives him the clarity to recognize a number of things: 1. Kazdin almost always picks a fight after seeing his mom. 2. Kazdin is hungry and tired. 3. He did not model coping with emotions very well for his son. 4. He was not responsive to Kazdin's pain.

As he thinks, he settles down. Later he goes looking for Kazdin in his room. He appears in his doorway and, in a calm tone, asks if he can come in and talk. Kazdin tentatively lets him in, and Dad can tell this conversation could go south with any wrong move. He says, "Son, I just want you to know that I am sorry for the comment I made about your mom. She loves you but doesn't always show it well. I know that hurts your feelings and might even make you sad. I know your visits can be difficult because they probably remind you of this. Would you agree?" Kazdin shares a little about his sadness, and Dad listens. Dad reminds Kazdin how important he is to him, and although he does not always get parenting right, he really loves him and is here when he needs him. Kazdin doesn't say anything, but his eye contact tells Dad he hears him and is taking it all in.

Here's what this feedback loop looks like.

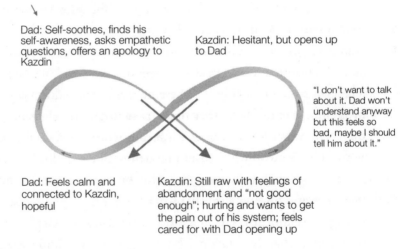

Dad: Self-soothes, finds his self-awareness, asks empathetic questions, offers an apology to Kazdin

Kazdin: Hesitant, but opens up to Dad

"I don't want to talk about it. Dad won't understand anyway but this feels so bad, maybe I should tell him about it."

Dad: Feels calm and connected to Kazdin, hopeful

Kazdin: Still raw with feelings of abandonment and "not good enough"; hurting and wants to get the pain out of his system; feels cared for with Dad opening up

Kazdin's dad couldn't stop his outburst in the moment but was able to speak to his son later, when they were both calm, and repair the disconnection they both felt. It can be hard to go to our tween and offer an apology, own our part in the argument, and listen to them speak when we are not quite sure which emotion it will provoke inside of us. However, when we do this, not only are we reestablishing our connection with our tween, we are also modeling how to connect with others, take responsibility for our behavior, and repair a relationship when it breaks.

Sometimes we can stop an interaction from becoming toxic by interjecting, that is, applying the brakes. We may offer words of comfort and ask a question to express *I want to know you*. This slows down our tween. We may take a deep breath and name the feelings arising within us to slow ourselves down as well. With these interjections, we are using emotional awareness to be more present so that we can better understand what is happening and steer it in a better direction. (We'll return to emotional awareness in greater detail in Part Seven: I Want to Know You. It's fascinating what we can do with it to productively parent our tween.)

Let's look at a final, slightly different example: Here, a client I'll call Meghan and her mom have learned to interject to reduce the number of negative feedback loops they were having.

When Meghan feels herself getting upset, she asks Mom for five minutes to cool off; she uses "I feel _____ because _____" sentences. Mom listens and validates them with comments such as: "I see how that could make you feel that way" or "Oh, that's interesting, so you're saying..." These interventions reduce Meghan's inclination to pull back. They open up new conversations between them. Mom has learned to take a breath when she feels frustrated and not walk away, which is her tendency. She has also learned to model emotional awareness and calm by naming her feelings as they arise and finding ways that work for her to feel better, such as taking a deep breath, saying a quick prayer, asking Meghan questions about what she is talking about to gain a better understanding of where she's coming from, and reframing negative thoughts. For example, when the familiar feeling of being overwhelmed appears, she'll think: *There it is: I'm starting to feel overwhelmed again, but I won't go there. If I do, Meghan will shut down.* As a result, Meghan feels like Mom is with her, that she is not alone. This minimizes her anxiety.

Here's their feedback loop.

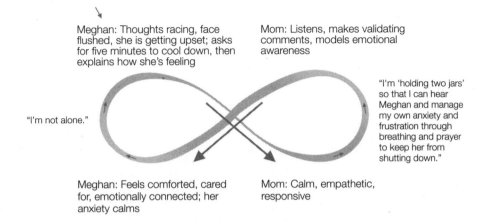

Meghan: Thoughts racing, face flushed, she is getting upset; asks for five minutes to cool down, then explains how she's feeling

Mom: Listens, makes validating comments, models emotional awareness

"I'm 'holding two jars' so that I can hear Meghan and manage my own anxiety and frustration through breathing and prayer to keep her from shutting down."

"I'm not alone."

Meghan: Feels comforted, cared for, emotionally connected; her anxiety calms

Mom: Calm, empathetic, responsive

Either you or your tween can interject, though tweens aren't good at slowing down and catching themselves in the middle of an escalating situation. They ride it. So it is more likely the interjecting will fall to you, which is more powerful and productive because of the additional opportunity it presents to show your tween how to be aware of their emotions, calm themselves, and put words to the experience. It will also add to their attachment experience and eventual style of attaching to others in important relationships. Remember, as central as peers are becoming to our tween, they're still very influenced by what we think, say, and do.

It's not about getting it perfect with our tween—that is an unrealistic bar to try to hit. The key is to be able to interject and slow down a negative feedback loop when we see things unraveling or repair an injury to our relationship when it happens.

Now that we have unpacked what feedback loops are and how they play out in relationships, we can start to be more intentional with things that happen quickly and unconsciously by being more aware of our emotions and steering our reactions in ways that support positive feedback loops with our tween. Remember the tween brain is pliable: With all that neuronal sprouting and pruning, this is the time to cultivate things we want the brain to keep and purge behaviors we want it to drop.

In the next section, I'll take you through tips and tools for effective parenting, probably the reason you picked up this book. We will look at what we have learned about emotional connection, the tween brain, our own soil issues (and remediating them) and feedback loops, and apply behavioral techniques that will help us build emotional connection—our bond with our tween.

QUESTIONS TO PONDER

1. Can you think of a memory where you felt safe, secure, known by others, valued in your family of origin? Can you see the feedback loop that occurred between you and a parent?

2. Pick a family member and draw out your feedback loop. Can you find a negative feedback loop and a positive feedback loop? Be sure to add your feelings, their feelings, and behavioral reactions for both of you. Likely there will be more than one behavior and feeling each.

SECTION TWO
INTRODUCTION

Your Toolbox: How to Use What You've Learned

As parents, we have a built-in care-giving system. We now know that. And, plainly, we love our children and want what's best for them. It is a powerful bond. But sometimes, our messages of love and care get lost, and emotional connection feels impossible. From the previous chapters, we now have the knowledge to understand the why of this: Perhaps it's a soil issue tripping us up or a disconnect over where our tween is developmentally. Maybe it's a feedback loop that has us trapped. This section gives us the how—the proven tips and tools to overcome these hurdles and connect with our tween, to uncover who they are and what they have done with our kid.

There are many options for building emotional connection with our tween. Some will work. Some won't. It depends on *your* relationship and who *you* and *your tween* are. Different things work for different people. So we watch for the winks and remember to go easy on ourselves if we fail to connect at first. We won't get it right 100 percent of the time. Nobody does. Start with one or two strategies. Sometimes parents try too many at once and become discouraged when they fail. Give each strategy several weeks at least to establish a pattern your tween can count on. Tweens, like most of us, are unlikely to buy something the first time they see it, so we keep at it.

Consistency also builds emotional memories. They become pathways in our tween's brain that say *I can count on my parents*, *My parents know me*, *My parents like me*. Time also gives us the opportunity to practice and modify each strategy as needed so that it feels right for us and our tween. Most importantly, we must be true to ourself. If we are not authentic, our tween will smell it, which will compromise their trust and, consequently, their interest in connecting.

Often in therapy, parents express frustration with the process because they feel like it won't work, it gives too much power to their tween, and they worry it will make the situation worse than what they started with. The truth is, we're learning a new language, and as with any new endeavor, it takes effort, understanding, patience, and commitment. But it will be worth it.

When it gets hard for me (yes, even the experts can struggle with this stuff!), I know that when I fall, God will carry me. When my kids fall, He will carry them. And so, I walk forward, with God in my heart, mind, and soul, confident in the strength, patience, and love He is giving me to guide my parenting.

Finally, it is important to note that the goal of emotional connection isn't to change who we are as parents to fit our tween, nor is it to give our tween the run of the house. Rather, it is to make sure our tween registers that we want to know the person they are becoming, that we are there to support them when they are struggling, celebrate them when they succeed, and still set the rules and boundaries that are so critical for them to grow into resilient, confident, caring adults…who may actually still want to come home to see us from time to time!

PART SIX

I See You

Care Magnified: It Starts Here

"While the days of parenting may seem so long,
the years are so short."

—DANIEL J. SIEGEL, MD, PSYCHIATRIST,
EXECUTIVE DIRECTOR OF MINDSET INSTITUTE

"Gentleness and self-control.
Against such things there is no law."

—GALATIANS 5:23 NIV

Early in my career, I was working with a nine-year-old girl who was talking back to her mom and pushing back on "the rules." As a rookie clinician, I started with reinforcing the boundaries and explaining why they are important. That went nowhere. Then I moved into consequences, what happens when she doesn't follow the rules. I could feel myself losing her interest. Eventually she burst out in pure frustration, "I am who I am!" I paused, somewhere between stunned and tickled by her comment and her strength to put it out there like that, and I wondered, "And who might that be?!" I asked her what she meant, and she shared how she felt about rules, what made her so angry, what she thought of her mom, and what she wanted from her mom. As I listened, I realized that this tween had an entire story about who she was, what she needed, and why, and I was completely missing it! I was focusing instead on her mom—the parent, and on her authority. How could I ever understand this tween if I didn't first "see" her?

The best thing we can give our tween is a platform to be seen: We must show up. They need to know that we *see them*, the same way God sees us with His focused attention—as worthy and loved, just as we are—gifts, flaws, and all. No judgment.

When we see our tween in this way, we can start to understand them, we can see them trying their hardest even if it falls short and still show our love for them. We can see the beauty in it. If we can take this first step to understand our tween, the rest will fall into place. If we don't make the effort to see them, they will check out.

Seeing our tween gives them time and space to develop a good understanding of themselves and practice putting words to their thoughts by hearing themselves think out loud. We see our tween through active listening, appreciating their perspective (even if it is wacky), and learning about the person they are becoming. We don't cut them off, talk over them, get mad, or divert the conversation to our agenda.

While "seeing" my tween, I do my best to be aware of *my* feelings and then hold them apart from our conversation so that I can be available to my tween. (This is the time for the jars we discussed in Part Four: Remediating Our Soil). If we're tired, overworking, drinking every night, or overwhelmed by stress in our life, we are going to have trouble actively listening and being open to what our tween has to say. However, when we protect the space around our tween, setting aside whatever we may be feeling, our tween feels *seen and respected.* The respect we give *them* is reflected in the respect they show *other people* in their life. To everyone all the time? No, and mostly to people when we're not around! We may hear about it from other adults. And when people tell us nice things about our sons and daughters, we know our listening has led to their kindness and caring for others. That is one of the best compliments a parent can receive! What's more, the respect we show our tween *builds their confidence and their assertiveness,* which also spills into their interactions with others.

So let's look at how we actively listen to really *see* our tweens, to show them we want to know the ideas, thoughts, and interests of the person they are becoming. Some of these tips may seem obvious but don't underestimate how important they are, and believe it or not, parents miss them more often than not.

CHAPTER SEVENTEEN

BEWARE THE PULL TO MULTITASK

Slow down. With the millions of things going on each day, finding time to connect and be together can be difficult. Our day may begin with a rush to get out the door—to school and work. Next might come a whole range of after-school activities for tweens and work or chores until dinner. We may enjoy (or not) a quick meal together, with our tween fleeing to their room or screens immediately after it ends. Then there are baths, showers, homework, and countless other tasks in a rush to bedtime—all distractions from parent–tween time.

By slowing down and giving our tween *undivided attention*, we send a message: *I want to know about your life. You are important.* It also gives *them* an opportunity to slow down and practice feeling part of something bigger than themselves—their family.

When we slow down, we get involved with what our tween is interested in. It could be sitting down next to them, turning off the television and electronic distractions and *really* listening. It could be watching them play Xbox or playing the game with them while we chat. Our tween may talk about something that sounds weird, boring, or trivial to us. Or they may be extremely upset or want to show us something that isn't interesting to us. They may have trouble putting words to what they are trying to share with us or be hard to talk to because they are uncomfortable sharing or seem uninterested in together time. Maybe they want to read quietly together side by side before bed or want us to sit with them while they babble as they wind down in their room and get ready for bed. We have to be patient. Take it all in. Follow. Let them guide the process. If we're paying attention, this is where we get a glimpse into who they are, what they think about, what intrigues them. And remember: They are looking for reassurance from us that they make sense.

Because we're busy with many demands on our time, we'll almost always want to multitask and half listen. Rarely does this work. We all think we can continue a repetitive job while we listen: We cannot. Tweens are extremely sensitive to others' perception of them, as we learned in Part Two: It's Not You, It's Neuroscience. They may misread our signals and conclude we are not interested in them.

When our tween comes in the room whining, talking, complaining, hopping around, they are looking for something—conversation, connection, fun, food, sleep. Something may be upsetting them. Or they may simply want to talk about school that day.

Ideally, *lean in*. Be curious about them and what they are saying or doing. You'll learn a lot about what your tween is thinking or questioning. This simple act of listening for verbal clues and watching for nonverbal messages is subtle but powerful. Ask three questions about what they are talking about. See if you can summarize what they said or how they are feeling.

I've found snack time right after school as well as the last half hour of the day to have the best potential for good conversation and sharing ideas, thoughts, and feelings with my tween. Other families create time to talk as they walk the dog together, drive to activities, relax right after dinner, work on a project together, or throw a ball. Find what fits you and your tween uniquely and authentically.

You will know you are slowing down and connecting with your tween by their facial expressions and tone of voice. They will smile, make eye contact, ask questions, answer questions, ask for a back scratch, laugh, share information, tease you, or just simply hang around you. And they will come back again for more time. Here's an example: A client I'll call Allison began pestering her mother about five p.m. every day, just as she started making dinner. With her attention on getting the meal on the table, Mom couldn't take time to sit with her.

Try This: Time Out

1. In your daily routine, find a specific time to be with your tween alone. Put your tween ahead of any work you may think you have to accomplish. It won't take as long as you think, and it's time well spent.

2. Take a moment right now to envision yourself coming home and going into a room where your tween is. Imagine the sound of the door opening and you walking in. Hear the sounds of the house. Feel the pull to start getting things done. Now imagine that happy flutter in your stomach. You smile, look for your tween, and join them in their activity. It's been all day since you saw them and you look forward to knowing what they experienced while you were apart.

3. Give yourself permission to clear your mind of other activities, thoughts, deadlines, and obligations. You are in the presence of your pride and joy, the object of your desire for parenthood.

4. Come up with your scenario to release your tension and preoccupation with your own life. Think about what calms you and makes you open to your tween.

Extra points if you write it down! Writing anything down slows the mind and increases your awareness of what you are experiencing or communicating. You can refer back to it later for inspiration or to see patterns over time.

One day, she asked Allison to help. She gave her a pot of pasta to stir, which gave them time to talk. It became a regular thing. By assigning Allison simple kitchen tasks, the two looked forward to this daily interaction as positive, rather than a negative interruption in which Allison felt she was competing for Mom's attention. It also gave them something to do together, a common goal. Allison felt part of the process, her mother heard all about her school day and issues, and Allison turned out to be a good chef!

Make Eye Contact

It is always amazing to me to see how often we *all* skip eye contact or never even consider it. It is so easy, yet parents and tweens default to talking to each other from across a room, while they're doing something else, or between rooms, shouting from one to another, rarely looking directly at each other. We miss such a simple opportunity to connect.

Eye contact is one of the most powerful ways to send messages of pleasure and reassurance. Our parents taught us to shake hands and look a person directly in the eye when greeting them to establish a good connection. The same is true with our tween.

A meeting of the eyes implies we see our tween and are curious about them, that we want to hear and see what they are saying and doing. You know how you feel when someone stops working and looks you in the eye? Imagine how good our insecure or anxious tween feels when we look directly at them while they talk.

Watch how they respond to eye contact. They may feel uncomfortable or self-conscious at first, especially if they are not used to the attention, but they will also feel important, seen—like their voice matters. It shows we are listening. It shows we care. Even if they don't like it at first, keep at it.

When they resist eye contact, there may be something else going on. For example, tweens will not look us in the eye when they feel they will be judged or criticized. If we only use eye contact with our tween when we are about to discuss something we're concerned or unhappy about, they will equate it with *Oh no, trouble*, rather than, *I see you and I love you*. We can fix this by striving to make eye contact in every situation, not just when they are in trouble, and by including a smile, a question, or a phrase of empathy when our eyes meet.

Tweens may also avoid eye contact if they are lying or feeling embarrassed or ashamed about something. If you sense this, slow down, look them in the eye, and ask questions. Hear their story. This reassures our tween that their voice matters. The slow pace keeps emotions from overflowing into an argument. Even if a boundary is imminent, we give them a chance to think through their actions if we listen to what they have to say about their wrongdoing. Ultimately, this helps them make better decisions in the future.

Try This: Aye Eye

Keep track of how often you talk to your tween or partner from another room, a doorway, as they are leaving a room, or while you are multitasking. Note the number of times you actually look at them when you are speaking. Next, observe how often your tween or partner makes eye contact with you when *they* are talking. What did you notice? What are you communicating? Does it feel different?

CHAPTER EIGHTEEN

WATCH THOSE FACIAL EXPRESSIONS, THAT BODY LANGUAGE, AND TONE OF VOICE

Once we have our tween's attention, we want to make the most of it. Parents universally encounter times when we become frustrated or angry and struggle to hold back our own emotional reaction while keeping our caregiver system intact. It can make empathy or even the desire to stay and talk with our tween really hard. This often shows up in the messages we send through our facial expressions, body language, and tone of voice. Intention is not always as important or the same as interpretation. In other words, the way *we take in messages* is what leads to hurt feelings, but does not necessarily reflect what *the messenger meant to say*. The way you or your tween interpret the message becomes—to the nervous system—the felt experience and results in certain behaviors.

Facial Expressions: The Many Things They Say

Facial expressions have a profound impact on the relationship we're able to build with our tween. They can instantaneously transmit *I am open to what you have to say* or *You are in trouble*, or *I don't like what you are saying*.

Acknowledging the power of facial expressions is a first step toward being mindful of their effect.

These unspoken responses to emotions triggered by interactions with our tween can leave us emotionally disconnected: They may as well be words! For example, tight lips, widening eyes, a tense brow, a frown, and eye rolls activate the part of our nervous system that reads a situation as dangerous, and we reach for a behavior to protect ourselves. Envision this: Our tween enters a room with a scowl on their face. Our defenses go up in anticipation of the argument or negotiation that is sure to follow. Or perhaps we enter a room flushed, a look in our eye that tells our tween they are in trouble (whether or not our look is even about them). Their nervous system clicks in. They feel the danger. They feel insecure. They're ready to fight to shut all those uncomfortable feelings down.

Try This: Look This Way

1. Look in a mirror and frown, draw in your eyebrows, tighten your lips, etc. Keep in mind this is what your tween sees and reacts to, picking up messages you might not intend such as *They don't think I'm capable* or *I am a burden.*

2. Look in the mirror and learn how you appear when you are upset. Practice softening your expression to a look that says, *I am here listening and trying to understand.* If you notice facial tensing, make a conscious effort to relax. Here are some ways to do that:
   • Pull your eyebrows upward once to reset them.
   • Relax your forehead.
   • Open your mouth to reset tense lips, making them fuller.
   • Blink to minimize eye rolls and eye widening.

Conversely, facial expressions can also communicate closeness or acceptance. We can catch and affirm something they said that was interesting with a smile and raised eyebrows. The bottom line is this: When we are aware of our facial expressions and use them intentionally, we can set the stage for emotional connection and the more open communication that comes with it.

Body Language Speaks Volumes

With facial expressions comes body language. We can see an argument start as danger, and that immediately registers in our nervous system. It plays out in physical responses: Our skin may redden, we might wave our hands, point a finger toward our tween's room, clench our fists, stand up tall, bounce out of our chair, or move quickly. Our tween may stomp their feet, cry, slam a door, run out of the room, puff up or take an aggressive stand in our personal space, or follow us around the house as we try to remove ourselves. Note that our tween isn't trying to be disrespectful or rude per se. Rather, they don't know how to interpret what is going on. *Nor can they maintain calm when faced with worry or the possibility they are in trouble, so they fight or flee.*

Body language, like facial expressions, can also be a tool to build emotional connection if we are intentional about it. For example, we can match our tween's position: If they are sitting, we sit. If they are standing at a counter, we stand at the counter. We can give them space by standing close enough to be in conversation but not so close that we're threatening. We can hold their hand, go in for a hug, cuddle (yes, they will still cuddle), high five, fist pump, nudge them on the shoulder, jump up with enthusiasm, or lean toward them to signal our desire to really listen to them.

We can be aware of our hand motions; we can move at a measured pace. This will keep our tween from feeling intimidated. We can be aware of our body movements when a conversation begins to escalate: If we tap our fingers, bite our nails, cross our arms, or tense our muscles, we will appear defensive and angry, and our tween will interpret it as danger—that we think they are wrong; that we are judging them; that we don't like them.

We can calm our body by resetting it through deep, slow breathing, by changing our position to sit or stand, or through tense-and-release exercises such as dropping our ear to our shoulder, holding it for two seconds then releasing it, clenching and releasing our fists, or moving our neck slowly, stretching one side then the other. Note: While these techniques might calm us, doing them in front of our tween could intimidate or make our tween nervous. We should evaluate whether our tween can tolerate them. If not, it is best to excuse ourselves and take them to another room.

Try This: Stop Signs

1. Note your facial expression and body language and your tween's as well. These are often the first clues that your tween feels danger or discomfort. With them comes a chance to stop an argument before it starts. You can, for example, take a deep breath. This will send oxygen through your bloodstream and get your blood circulating—a cleansing, calming process. It also injects a quiet moment to slow down your stress response (and your tween's). When we are calmer, our body language and facial expression are softer and more inviting. Observe how your tween reacts.

2. Say both you and your tween are past the point of preempting a disagreement. Your anger, annoyance, frustration, and body language have put the danger you feel in your nervous system on full display. See if you can tell where you hold the tension in your body, then bring blood flow to the area through tense-and-release exercises. Observe how this changes the conversation.

As we learned in Part Five: Dancing Neurons, if we are calm, we communicate calm to our tween, even as they experience a storm inside. How we carry our body will pace the conversation. It allows us to become more intentional about what we're doing and rein in the heated emotions we may be feeling. It gives our tween space to gather themselves. At a less-charged time, we can talk to our tween about tensing and relaxing muscles and other ways to defuse a tense moment. Then, in a stressed moment, our tween might try one of them or see us doing it. Just seeing and understanding the movement might inject some much-needed humor into our exchange or stop a conflict outright.

Tone of Voice: The Power of Pitch

Words are important, but tone is even more critical. This sounds so basic but, like eye contact, facial expression, and body language, tone of voice is often underestimated. Yet it has such command over our relationship with our tween. It can send a strong message of pleasure, or pain, tapping those emotional memories between us that are responsible for the reactions that come most immediately to us. Even a slight change in tone can make a big difference by activating the stress response or producing a safe, soothing, and comforting feeling. The voice is a powerful tool.

How would you describe your neutral voice tone? When upset, do you tend to speak in a loud, high-pitched, sharp tone or a lower, deeper tone? Perhaps you say nothing at all. (Silence is a tone of voice too.) Do you talk fast or barely speak, relying on facial expressions? A father's voice is usually louder than a mother's, and fathers need to realize this when speaking to their tween. If a tween is yelling, yelling back only escalates the interaction, often leading to words we regret later.

In contrast, if we speak firmly and ask a question directly or make a statement, it can stop our tween's emotional trajectory and start to soothe their nervous system, especially if we add a softer facial expression and less threatening body language.

Try This: Tone Up

In a peaceful moment, play this game with your tween: Tell them you want to try different voice tones and see how they feel about them. They must be honest and tell you exactly what thought comes to mind when they hear that tone. You may be surprised what they say. Ask your tween to try different tones of voice on you. Tell them what comes to mind for you with each one.

These simple tips make a huge difference in showing our tween that we truly care about them. In fact, they are among the most powerful things we can do to help them feel the calm and comfort they need to communicate with us. And each time we smile, make eye contact, etc., we are planting seeds that will lead us to be closer—emotionally connected—to our tween. What's more, by expressing their thoughts out loud, our tween starts to develop critical thinking ability, gain courage to voice their thoughts, and build on concepts they believe in—all part of a valuable skill set they will use throughout their lives.

QUESTIONS TO PONDER

1. If you completed some of the "try this" exercises, what did you notice in your tween's body language, tone, or facial expressions when they were upset? Nervous? Happy?

2. Which of these tips seem to work best with your tween?

3. Which of these tips seem the most difficult for you to try?

4. When is the best time for you to slow down with your tween? What can you do to slow the pace?

PART SEVEN

I Want to Know You

Drilling Down to Build
Emotional Connection

"Children do not always connect or reconnect easily.
They may feel so isolated that they retreat into a corner or come
aggressively with both arms swinging. They may be annoying,
obnoxious, or downright infuriating as they try desperately to signal
to us that they need more connection. These situations call
for creating more playtime, not doling out punishment
or leaving the lonely child alone."

—LAWRENCE COHEN, PSYCHOLOGIST

"Don't just pretend to love others. Really love them.
Hate what is wrong. Hold tightly to what is good.
Love each other with genuine affection,
and take delight in honoring each other."

—ROMANS 12:9–10 NLT

t's one thing to *see* our tween. It's quite another to make sure they know we really want to *know* them as well. This means working to understand how they view their world by interacting with them—asking them questions, factoring in how they may be feeling based on their actions, and teaching them how to recognize, process, and express their emotions—to read between the lines and decipher what they're *truly* communicating. This is your path to discovering *Who Are You and What Have You Done with My Kid.*

Tweens say and do all sorts of things that are inaccurate, emotionally driven, hard to decipher, and just plain lies. Sometimes they tell us what they think we want to hear and not what actually happened. Other times they tell us what they think will get them in the least amount of trouble or bring the biggest reward. They may share something they heard on TikTok or what another kid said. They are testing humor and different points of view; they're experimenting with selling their agenda; they're exploding emotionally without much thought, and they don't have a good sense of how to cope with their big emotions such as insecurity, embarrassment, and anger (as you will recall from Part Two: It's Not You, It's Neuroscience). It's all impulsive trial and error. They think and behave at the same time they're trying to figure out how to deal with their world.

For parents, it is very easy to jump to challenge errors and correct them, give answers, provide solutions, finish their sentences, shorten the conversation, reframe their viewpoint to something more positive, leap to discipline, or even explode, matching their emotions with our own. However, getting caught up in details or inaccuracies—the *literal* story they are telling—sidetracks us from understanding what our tween is *actually* trying to communicate. This can lead to misunderstanding and conflict. We can wind up shaming our tween, invalidating what they are feeling, punishing them when they are struggling, and demolishing their confidence when it's the last thing we mean to do!

Here's how it can play out: The other day, a client shared a conversation between her and her tween. "My daughter said, 'Mom, I think I might want to try out for gymnastics. Bella is going to do it.' I stopped her right there and told her she can't try out for gymnastics because her friend is doing it. I told her she has to look for things she wants to do which is why she should think about the chorus group, something she has always done."

How We Butt In

What We Say	What Our Tween Hears
Let me stop you right there…	You are wrong.
I think you should…	I am going to solve the problem for you.
You just need to…	My way works, your way doesn't.
Yeah, but…	What you're saying isn't important.
I understand what you're saying but…	I'm not listening to you.
That's not really how it went…	You don't know what you're talking about and it wasn't as big a deal as you think it was.

Mom thought she was helping her daughter learn to think independently. In truth, not only did my client assume she knew what her daughter was thinking and miss a moment to learn something new about her, she lost the opportunity to help her daughter think through how she felt about gymnastics and her motives for wanting to participate. She also gave her daughter *her* agenda, which put her daughter in the place of knowing her mom's preference and either going with it or picking something that might not be as acceptable to mom, setting them up for a potential argument or drifting. If our tween feels like we won't like their decisions, they may equate it with us not liking them, and they very well may stop sharing.

Here's another way to think about it: When you go into the ocean and a wave is coming, what do you do? I frequently ask parents this. Their answers?

"Wait for it to pass."
"Run to the shore."
"Try to swim through it."
"Turn my back."

No, no, no! You *dive under the wave*. It takes you deeper into the ocean, where it is calm and quiet. You can see the sun shining through the water. It is the other side of the rush of intense water and potential danger of the wave. That's exactly what listening to a tween is like. If we take our tween's words literally, we can get swooped up into misunderstanding and calling them out on their lies, confusion, and inaccuracies, leaving us both frustrated and beaten by the wave. If we work to understand the meaning of what they're saying within the context of their bigger experience, we enter the undercurrent of their thinking and emotions: Are they working out something from their day? Their words and actions may look and sound like anger, but they may actually be masking embarrassment. Our tween may yell at us and blame us for something minor when they are actually wishing they could tell us we disappointed them or they miss us because we've been working a lot lately. Or it may be they are struggling with harder issues such as trouble learning, anxiety, or depression. Or they may feel we're rushing them to say what they're thinking and can't figure out how to translate their thoughts to words as quickly as we're pressing them to do it.

As you will also recall, our tween's ability to think and communicate is still under development; tying words to feelings, thoughts, and experiences is difficult. They don't know how to process and make sense of it all yet, let alone explain it. And if they can't understand it or explain it, imagine how hard it is to come up with the right actions and words on demand.

That's where we come in: There is so much we can do to help our tween make sense of their undercurrents by listening to their thoughts, asking questions, wondering about them, letting them do the hard work of thinking and talking. We can then get to the root of how they feel and what they're actually trying to say.

Here is an example of what I mean: A tween client of mine got a

COVID shot. On the way home, his mom talked on the phone about diseases and preventive shots with a friend. When they reached home, my client started to whine and withdraw. When Mom sat down with him and asked him questions rather than correcting what appeared to be annoying behavior, she dove under the wave. He confessed he was worried about the COVID shot and all the side effects he had heard her mention to her friend. They talked about his fears and how the COVID shot would actually prevent him from having to deal with the serious effects of an illness. He asked many questions, and when she didn't know all the details, the two researched answers on the internet. After just ten minutes, his mood changed, and the parent–child connection was restored. Had she simply told him, "Stop whining," she would have been caught in the wave.

When we help our tweens understand their emotions and cope with them rather than butt in, they feel our patience and acceptance. They will trust us when they are vulnerable. They will feel safe with us. *They will feel emotionally connected to us.* Giving them space to talk also purges emotion and helps them feel better, clearing the way for better communication and a more positive relationship with us. It gives them a chance to practice self-expression. And every time we do this, we are building their emotional life skills, also known as emotional intelligence. (Yes! This can be taught.)

This is where faith steps in with a huge assist. Have you ever felt a shift in your emotions, against all reason, one that takes you to a place of calm just as you are about to blow in a destructive direction...a sense of peace that restores your rationality? I call this grace, the kind that comes from God and our certainty that He is with us every second of every day, reminding us of the gifts our tweens are and leading us to be good stewards of them. It is the same grace that helps us teach our tweens to know their emotions, express them, and cope with them so they feel good about themselves and emotionally connected to us...and it's available to everyone. With God's grace in our corner, we proceed.

CHAPTER NINETEEN

TRANSLATING
THE UNDERCURRENTS:
EMOTIONAL INTELLIGENCE

A cornerstone of understanding our undercurrents is emotional intelligence (EI) and the tween years are when our kids start to develop it.

The term *emotional intelligence* first appeared in 1964 in a paper written by Cornell University psychologist Michael Beldoch. The first model of EI was developed by psychologists John Mayer and Peter Salovey (now president of Yale University). However, EI didn't fully penetrate the public mindset until the 1990s when psychologist and author Daniel Goleman published the bestseller *Emotional Intelligence: Why It Can Matter More Than IQ*. He spelled out EI as the ability to:

- Practice self-awareness.
- Recognize, understand, and manage emotions to cope.
- Empathize and interact positively with other people.

Tweens who learn about emotional intelligence will have more self-control during difficult or stressful situations when they are older because they understand their emotions better. They will be more adaptable and make better decisions. They will be less disruptive when emotions run hot.

They will be able to be a better friend and classmate. They will be less likely to be overwhelmed by negative thoughts and emotions. They will handle academic challenges better. Over time, this will build self-confidence and a willingness to operate outside their comfort zone. Plainly, the more emotional intelligence our child develops, the easier it is to parent the teen our tween becomes.

But because our tween is at the beginning of their road to emotional intelligence, it can be awkward. It's like teaching them to lift weights. At first they will mishandle the weights as they try different ways to hoist them. Eventually they will develop the proper form and muscle memory that will ultimately make the lift reflexive. In a similar way, as we start to teach our tween emotional intelligence, we may see some pretty goofy behavior. My son overheard me ask my husband, "What's coming up for you?" and asked, "Mom, why do you always say that to Dad?" I replied, "I ask him this because I want to help him sort out what he is going through." Later, when his four-year-old sister was melting down, he asked, "Livvy, what's coming up for you?" He realized her emotional outburst had meaning but how goofy...a four-year-old? Really? Also, not for nothing, his insight bit the dust when I asked him later, mid-meltdown of his own, "What's coming up for you?" His reply? "Don't talk to me!" Okay, so he wasn't able to apply it to himself, but he will. Eventually.

> ## The Qualities of Emotional Intelligence
>
> - Self-awareness
> - Self-control
> - Self-motivation
> - Social skills
> - Patience
> - Empathy

EI at School

If you see social emotional skills groups or other curriculum offerings in your school or community, support them, promote them, encourage them, vote for them, and have your tween participate in them. These curricula aim to teach tweens to be more emotionally intelligent—to empathize with others and be patient with differences, to understand and manage their own feelings so they can perform to the best of their ability academically and relationally.

Building Emotional Intelligence

Spot It—Emotional Awareness
Say It—Emotional Expression
Rule It—Emotional Regulation

Emotional intelligence has three parts: 1. Recognizing and understanding emotion (emotional awareness); 2. Communicating emotion (emotional expression); and 3. Controlling emotion (emotional regulation). I think of it as *Spot It, Say It, Rule It.*

CHAPTER TWENTY

SPOT IT
(EMOTIONAL AWARENESS)

Some tweens blow their top. Others hold it all in. Others become anxious or withdrawn. Most tweens are some combination of these, though they typically gravitate to one behavior more often than another. Regardless, all of it points to the flood of emotion they are experiencing and how unsure they are about what to do with it. To help them develop the emotional intelligence they need to manage their strong emotions, we must first help them identify and understand what they are feeling. This is called emotional awareness.

Emotions are quick, reactive, and instinctual, (which is why it is difficult to just change an emotion on command). Each of us—including our tween—has our own subjective experiences with emotions and an internal dialogue about them. Emotional awareness is about recognizing and understanding this. It includes:

- Acknowledging that emotions are perfectly normal.
- Recognizing emotions in what our body is doing.
- Putting words to emotions.

Make It Normal

One of the best things we can do for our tween is help them understand that emotions are natural, everyone has them—the happy, the sad, the light, the heavy. They are part of life, and there is as wide a range of emotions as there are experiences to react to. This is where emotional awareness begins. We want to make sure our tween knows that it is okay to feel angry, sad, overwhelmed, or anxious, and to feel happy, calm, and confident. We should be grateful for the trickier emotions we have. They give us a chance to drop in deeper as human beings and make our lives more interesting.

We won't be able to control our emotions all the time nor change them immediately. But we can spot them, understand them, talk about them, and decide how to respond to them. When we send the message that feelings are normal, we teach our tweens *they* are normal—no matter what they may be going through. And regardless of whether or not they have a propensity toward anger, depression, anxiety, etc., it's what we *do* with our emotions that matters.

Body of Knowledge

As we know from Part Four: Remediating Our Soil, emotions can be measured in physical changes—our blood pressure, breathing, adrenaline and energy levels, focus, and heart rate. We can *see* our emotions in our body language and facial expressions. We can *hear* them in our tone of voice and the words we choose, if we are aware.

Emotional awareness is rooted in self-awareness: We notice something is happening in our body and take time to be curious about it. It is the first step toward learning to build positive responses to negative emotions. This is the beginner version of what we covered in Part Four. (What we teach our tween is prevention. The steps we take with ourselves are intervention.)

To help our tween understand *what* they're feeling, we can ask *how* they are feeling. See if they equate racing thoughts and a pounding heart

Body of Proof

Physical Signs of Strong Emotions

- Pounding heart
- Sweaty palms
- Hot face
- Inability to focus/ racing thoughts
- Stomachache
- Headache
- Low energy
- Negative thinking
- Emotional eating
- No appetite
- Extra sleeping
- Insomnia/not sleeping enough

with anxiety, or a hot face and adrenaline rush with anger, or low energy and avoiding their peers with depression, disappointment, or sadness. Being aware of what happens in their body and putting a name to it gives them a way to make sense of their reaction. Remember from Part Two: It's Not You, It's Neuroscience, the nervous system is attached to the entire body, so when the limbic system has an emotion, the body feels it.

Name That Feeling

We name the emotions we experience as feelings. Feelings cannot be measured. They can only be described. When our tween puts words to the feelings their emotions are triggering, they start to learn the very complicated and powerful process of self-awareness. As you may also recall from Part Two, tweens have a lot of emotions—many they've not felt before—and, as we've reiterated, they lack the words to articulate them. They are embarrassed and often self-conscious talking about their thoughts, because they fear they might explain them poorly or get the wrong reaction. They're in uncharted waters, and they feel insecure. As a result, many tweens won't even try to talk about any of this. Rather, they hope, *If I don't talk about it, maybe it will go away or stop.*

So we must help them attach words to their emotions by offering suggestions for what they could be feeling. For example, we might say:

- "I wonder if you were embarrassed by what the teacher said to you in front of the class."

- "You were really angry earlier when we spoke in your room. Are you still that mad or are you frustrated?"
- "I can see you're really sad."
- "I love how proud you are about your grade. You worked hard for that."
- "Your coach gave you a really nice compliment about your performance. Does that feel good to hear?"
- "You tried that. It was really hard and you did well. Do you feel the accomplishment of challenging yourself and coming out the other side?"
- "What a good life lesson; you tried something hard and although it didn't turn out like you wanted, do you think you learned a couple things along the way? That must feel good, no?"

Being able to name different emotions through feelings words steers our tween to notice their emotions with curiosity rather than shame, fear, uncertainty, or anxiety. When they have a word for what they're feeling, they can make sense of themselves and be understood by others.

Plus, as they name their feelings, we can show our tween empathy with statements such as:

- "Wow, I'm glad you told me that, I didn't realize."
- "Oh, I had no idea you felt that way. That makes a lot of sense."
- "This stuff is hard to talk about. You're doing a good job."
- "I appreciate you sharing that with me."
- "This is tough stuff you're going through. What would be helpful to talk about?"

Our empathy gives them reassurance.

The Feelings Chart

I have found tweens love the Feelings Chart. I ask them to circle the emotions they had throughout the day. I love the Feelings Chart because the top line names the emotion most commonly expressed followed by a list of related emotions that get to the nuance of what they are feeling. It's very validating. Think about it: *I'm angry* doesn't feel nearly as good as *I feel provoked.* It is amazing how often people (both kids and adults) will say, *I'm angry* when what they're really feeling is ignored, which, of course, is much more about hurt feelings than anger. Interestingly, the first time I present the feelings chart, most of my clients seem uninterested. However, very soon thereafter, it's their go-to. The reason is, when they find their word, their soul tells them: That's it! And in the knowing, they feel relief.

Happy Feelings	Sad Feelings
Glad	Regretful
Pleased	Unhappy
Playful	Gloomy
Cheerful	Blah
Content	Embarrassed
Confident	Quiet
Wanted	Worthless
Strong	Low
Special	Dreary
Wonderful	Discouraged
Proud	Moody
Generous	Gloomy
Relaxed	Shameful
Excited	Ashamed
Alive	Concerned
Hilarious	Dismal
Lighthearted	Grumpy
Caring	Sulky
Eager	Depressed
Festive	Somber
Joyous	In the dumps
Carefree	Sullen
Optimistic	Defeated
Thrilled	Down
Content	Hopeless
Satisfied	Remorseful

Angry Feelings	Hurt Feelings	Afraid Feelings	Misc. Feelings
Mad	Offended	Fearful	Envious
Impatient	Worried	Alarmed	Bored
Frustrated	Crushed	Threatened	Cooperative
Resentful	Ignored	Scared	Forgiving
Furious	Excluded	Guilty	Determined
Enraged	Inadequate	Distrustful	Loving
Hostile	Inferior	Trapped	Repulsed
Rebellious	Unwanted	Vulnerable	Encouraged
Defiant	Unloved	Uneasy	Tense
Sullen	Lonely	Uncomfortable	Feisty
Stubborn	Suffering	Terrified	Doubtful
Fuming	Despair	Insecure	Preoccupied
Irate	Heartbroken	Hesitant	Bold
Boiling	Injured	Suspicious	Tired
Bitter	Aching	Overwhelmed	Humble
Provoked	Pathetic	Timid	Fascinated
Upset	Neglected	Perplexed	Curious
Pushed	Degraded	Powerless	Creative
Irritated	Rejected	Worried	Hardy
Resentful	Isolated	Frightened	Jealous
Stubborn	Awful	Apprehensive	Mixed up
Belligerent	Cheated	Uncertain	Confused
Argumentative	Dejected	Shaky	Proud
Sulky	Disappointed	Panicky	Inquisitive
Indignant	Let down	Nervous	Alive
Grumpy	Miserable	Anxious	Shy

CHAPTER TWENTY-ONE

SAY IT
(EMOTIONAL EXPRESSION)

If emotional awareness is recognizing an emotion and putting a name to it, emotional expression is how we behave and share our thoughts based on the emotions we experience.

How we express our emotions can either draw people closer and invite the support we often need when dealing with emotional experiences or push people away. During the tween years, it's on us to teach our children how to express their emotions, to develop those ways of expressing themselves that will last a lifetime. Remember, as important as peers are becoming, parents are still the lead influence among tweens, and they *will* follow us.

Talk about It

There's no way our tween can express their emotions without talking. Obviously. But that's easier said than done with most tweens. It requires meeting them where they are and creating opportunities to talk.

Sometimes our tween will be too upset to talk about their experiences and feelings. Maybe they need a few minutes to cool off. Other times our tween won't talk at all and will need to be drawn out. Maybe they need to think through things on their own first. They are like cats, as you saw with

Caleb and his mom in Part Five: Dancing Neurons. You are never going to catch a cat if you chase it. You must wait. Don't move too fast. Watch. Eventually the cat will sit down next to us if we follow their lead.

Sometimes our tween's big emotions will be too much for *us* to handle, and we will have a hard time sitting with them. Consider the exercises in Part Four: Remediating Our Soil to find the head space where we can tolerate holding them and respond to their feelings. (Remember the jars: What's in our tween's jar and what's in ours?) We can share our feelings, perhaps saying something like, "This is tough, I can even feel myself getting upset. Know I'm not mad at you. It's just a tough situation and it's bringing up memories for me that have nothing to do with you," or "I hope you know I'm not mad at you. You didn't do anything wrong. I just have strong feelings about this, too. But I do want to hear more about what this is like for *you*."

If our tween is angry, we *must not* meet anger with anger or ultimatums. That is *not* meeting them where they are. It will only escalate the situation and make our tween feel more out of control, less secure. And if we tell our tween, "Just settle down," it's like asking them to go from seventy-five miles per hour straight into reverse. They are having an adrenaline rush full of cortisol (stress hormone), and we're demanding the mood-stabilizing hormone serotonin—the absolute opposite. We must stay calm ourselves, give them the time they need, but then definitely follow up. This lets our tween know they are important, their experiences matter. Most of this stuff they go through is not about a one-and-done conversation. It is a *series* of conversations over time. I remember my son being in a bad mood and I asked about it, got nothing. Later, I asked about it again, got nothing. I asked about it the next day, and he was able to talk about it. It took three times of me asking and letting him off the hook with "nothing." This gave him the opportunity to think through the situation and get to a point where he could talk about it. The trick is to keep asking but without demanding they talk or anxiously asking, asking, asking, asking, asking. Remember the cat!

Similarly, if our tween is retreating, we must not leave them alone.

We should sit with them, unpack what they are feeling, and show we care rather than leave them to fill the void by themselves. Some kids need help with language, and we can offer that using the tactics we covered above. We have to consider that some tweens are quieter, calmer, and more peaceful. It's just the way they are. They may not be going through anything at all. If our tween says nothing even after the kind of tactful follow-up described above, consider the possibility of phantom worry: Is there something really going on here, or could we be creating worry, perhaps out of our own soil issues?

Look for Patterns

When we listen to our tween, we can often see a common theme running through what they say. It could be a recurring feeling or thought, a problem with a friend.

As our tween talks, dive beneath that wave, look for patterns, and consider what might be going on in the bigger picture of their life. Then respond to the bigger emotions they may be having rather than to what's happening right now. Listen for any seemingly unrelated comments they make and what they might have in common: For example, if our tween focuses on how bad her grades are, how she doesn't own the hottest new thing, or how so-and-so "cool" kid called her out on a recent low test grade, look for the deeper meaning. Convincing her she has nice things is the wave. Explaining that if she studied harder or "solving" her distress by planning a study schedule or hiring a tutor for her could all miss what she may be trying to express. How she *really* feels most likely has nothing to do with a specific grade or clothes but rather with how inadequate or embarrassed she feels compared to her peer group. Instead, we might say, "Well I can only imagine if you don't feel like you are doing well in school or have the same pretty style, it's kind of a double hurt. And on top of it, a girl is calling you out about your grade *and* doing it in front of others? That is so embarrassing when you are trying to do well in school and here you have someone pointing out where you are struggling." We are linking the parts of the story that need to be addressed.

We can take them even deeper by asking questions such as, "Do you think you feel that way because of A, B, or C?" or "You've had this anger before when X happened; do you think this is related?" The more we do this with them the greater an understanding they develop of themselves. They learn over time to be aware of emotions, to understand them and what triggers them. They start to learn the difference between what is bothering them on the surface of their lives and the deeper meaning the experience has for them. They start to see patterns in their feelings, other people's behaviors, the choices they have…and it's empowering! They won't figure this out entirely until they are adults (and even then it may remain elusive), but this practicing puts them on the road to learning how to go deeper inside themselves over time.

What They See Is What They Say (Modeling)

Our tween sees much more than we realize: How *we* handle our emotions teaches them how to handle *their* emotions. Scary thought. It doesn't have to be, if we are aware of our own actions and what is driving our responses, and if we are honest about them with our tween in a way that is appropriate for where they are developmentally. How do we handle anger? Do we explode? Or do we stop, take a breath, calm ourselves? What do we do when we are sad? Do we retreat? Eat? Drink? Talk about it, face it, perhaps cry and move through it? All of this is tied to the soil issues we talked about in Part Three: What Lies Beneath.

When we acknowledge our own emotions and our tween sees that, we take normalizing emotions for them a step further. We teach them to be open and give them ideas for how to cope with and express *their* emotions. We do not need to point out that we are doing it. The example we set reinforces it far more than words could.

For example, if our tween sees us being moody—maybe our facial expressions are tight and our tone is tense or we are lethargic and withdrawn—and asks about it, we can name our emotion and talk about it in an age-appropriate way. For example, we might say, "It's nine p.m. and I am so exhausted. I can tell I have no patience left," or "April is the worst month for me at work, and I know I come home overwhelmed and have a hard time relaxing." This puts words to what our tween is watching us experience. Now they have an explanation for what they may otherwise assume reflects how we feel about them. (Remember how self-focused tweens are.) If we deny our moodiness, thinking we are sparing our tween, we unintentionally teach them not to trust their intuition.

Here's another example: If I'm angry and my tween asks me if I am and I say "No," I confuse him. He knows I'm angry. In denying it, I leave him to imagine all kinds of incorrect reasons for it.

Alternatively, we can also be proactive and share what is happening to us. For instance, we might say, "Yikes. It's almost nine p.m. I know I'm going to turn into a pumpkin (raging lunatic) in a few minutes, so I better get ready for bed." Or, "This month is going to be crazy busy. I have to figure out how to be overwhelmed and not take it out on you every night."

In modeling how we handle our emotions, we can also help them develop the same empathy for our emotions as we have for theirs. And yes, that comes over time. We have to be patient. (My son has learned *zero* empathy for me when I cry at a movie. He still gets irritated!)

When Your Tween Won't Talk

To get the conversation going, we can help our tween create a story by connecting *what* they are feeling to *how* it is affecting their body, how it led to their behavior, *and* what triggered the emotion in the first place. Tying a story to their feelings helps them understand *why* they may be feeling and behaving as they are.

In some cases, it might help to use personal experiences to relate to their emotion, such as, "I remember this time when I was your age these kids did X and I felt so humiliated. Have you ever felt that way?" As we tell our story, we teach our tween how we tie our own feelings to experiences. By asking them if they can relate to our story, we bring it back to them and their experience—something we must always do. (It reinforces with them just how much we want to know them.) Sometimes tweens like personal stories because they get to know us in a different *You were once a kid, too?!* way. Note: This can backfire. Tweens are at a stage where they think they are the only ones who have ever experienced this stuff. So sometimes, they can hear your stories and feel like they are not understood or minimized. You will need to find out how your tween handles your personal stories and proceed accordingly: Do they shut down? Do they light up?

The Now Dilemma

Sometimes our tween comes to us with an intense emotion or demand that must be addressed NOW. That need to connect might pass quickly; tweens don't do well being put on hold, so we don't want to miss it. But we all understand we can't always drop everything when they want. The world does not work like that. It is okay if they have to wait sometimes. (It's a bonus opportunity to teach delayed gratification.) What you can do is ask yourself, *Do I have the time to shelve what I'm doing and dig in for a long conversation?* or *Can I spare just five minutes to be completely present with my tween and find out what's up?* (Even knowing what you're signing up for helps you set your mind and intention to listen.) If you cannot stop what you are doing and fully focus on your tween, look at them (make eye contact) and say, "I have to finish this but let's connect at three p.m. or in ten minutes." Just be sure to set a specific time and honor it.

As our tween opens up to talking, using feelings words and tying them to what they experienced, we can offer a summary of what we are hearing. For example, we might say: "So, it sounds as if the kids stopped talking when you walked up to them, and you felt left out or insecure, is that right?" This gives us a chance to make sure we heard what they said correctly. It is also a way for us to give our tween more insight without telling them what their experience was. We can link additional thoughts or patterns related to their experience, even though they may not have talked about them. For example, if our tween is feeling disappointed about not doing well on a test, we might suggest, "I know you studied hard for that and are disappointed you didn't do better. Do you think you were hungry or tired during the test and maybe that hurt your concentration?" We may know this is the reason, that we are stating the obvious. But we lob it in there anyway, soft and easy: If we throw a fastball, they may never catch it.

CHAPTER TWENTY-TWO

RULE IT
(EMOTIONAL REGULATION)

Once our tween can name a feeling (emotional awareness) and think about different ways to communicate it (emotional expression), they can learn to rule it. Emotional regulation is about improving impulse control and moderating the intensity of our emotions. It is the third part of emotional intelligence.

Before we get any deeper into this section, it's important to keep in mind as we work to manage emotions step-by-step, that is, name them, express them, then regulate them, sometimes we're better at it than others. Becoming proficient is a lifelong journey—for everyone—and our tween is just starting to learn about it. So we want to honor their learning curve here and their courage to give it all a try. It's not easy, and regulating or ruling our emotions is often the hardest part, at any age. *Complicating it further, often emotional expression and emotional regulation happen simultaneously.* People want to react how they want to react. It's honest and authentic after all, right? Well, no. A puppy peeing in the house is authentic...but only because they don't know another way. Once a puppy is trained to go outside, the indoor peeing stops and everyone is happier. They go to the door because they *learn* to go to the door. It's the same with people: Emotional regulation can be learned.

The key to emotional regulation with our tween is to help them calm down—first by helping them identify the emotion they're feeling, including its intensity, then by helping them develop ways to moderate its force and the way they are expressing it, especially if the emotion is big. As you will see, most of this comes from our actions.

Scaling Emotional Intensity

One of the most effective strategies to measure the intensity of our emotions then manage them intentionally is the 1-to-10 scale we covered in Part Four: Remediating Our Soil. Not only is it useful in helping *us* remediate our soil issues, it is a key tool for teaching our tween how to regulate *their* emotions. This is about using it with our tween. As you recall: 1 to 3 are small emotions, 4 to 6 are the medium, more distracting emotions, 7 to 9 are the really big emotions that interfere with our ability to concentrate, 10 covers the extreme behaviors.

When I work with tweens, I ask them what types of things are on each part of their scale. They could be specific experiences such as *when my dad yells at me*, or more general things such as *when it is rainy*, or *when I don't like what is on the lunch menu*. I write this down with them. They have to buy into what they put on their scale, even if we don't agree with them. That's what matters most here.

Tipping the Scale

When our tween is at 1 to 3 on the scale, we are typically talking, exploring ways to express our emotions and keep them under control or regulated.

As you may also remember from Part Four, I call level 4 to 6 on the scale the bridge. It's when emotions are starting to heat up (anger is flaring or sadness is bringing them down). This is the best time to interject to slow the emotion, bring our tween back to the moment we are in, and tip the scale to stop them from crossing the bridge. Here's what we can do. Note: Once our tween crosses that bridge to 7 on the scale, their nervous system has released messages to their body, and now it is involved. At this point, we have to let the body run its course before we can intervene.

The Emotion Scale: What It Means for Our Tween

1 to 3 Small Emotions	4 to 6 The Bridge	7 to 9 Big Emotions	10 Extreme Behavior
Melancholy	Hurt	Depressed	School refusal
Upset	Disappointed	Shame	Complete avoidance
Shy	Embarrassed	Humiliation	Defiance
Eustress	Anxiety	Panic	Cutting
Confused	Amped up	Anger	Rage
Unsure	Confused	Overwhelmed	Suicidal

Pick times throughout the day to consider your emotional state. Name what you're feeling then decide its strength on a 1 to 10 scale. How strong are your emotions? Tracking your emotions over time gives a concrete, factual picture of them. Repeat this exercise with your tween. See what patterns emerge.

- **We can talk about it.**

  We can ask our tween to name the emotion and the trigger. Sometimes when our tween can find a way to express the emotion they're experiencing, they feel empowered, and it weakens its hold on them. (See the Feelings Chart on pages 192–193.) As we talk, we can slow the conversation—literally put the brakes on, use fewer words, and lower our voice.

- **We can stay calm.**

  Our tone of voice, facial expressions, body language, and undivided attention all matter immensely to how much our tween will share when they are in their most vulnerable moments and revving up on the emotional scale. Remember, most likely they are experiencing emotion with no understanding of what is going on for them. It is in these moments we must resist the pull of our own dysregulated emotions and use a softer tone, facial expressions, and body language. These will calm our tween and help them feel safe and heard.

- **We can use "Period. Pause."**

  This is a tactic I've shared with many clients, and they love it. It's a great way to put the brakes on any exchange that has landed us on the bridge. It works for us, and it works for our tween (though it may take more practice for them to remember to use it), and it's simple to do: When we or our tween get to the end of a sentence, say silently, "Period. Pause." and count to five. We don't need to respond immediately when our tween finishes talking. Pausing allows us to slow the emotional fire. It's amazing just how much it can do.

- **We can pace the conversation.**

  If we pace the conversation correctly, we can pull our tween off the bridge. Conversely, a difference in styles can derail our best efforts without us even realizing it. I remember a daughter and mother I worked with. The mom was full of life, high-energy, very excitable. When her daughter brought up a topic, she would talk fast and ask a lot of questions. You could see her interest and longing to know her tween. Her daughter, who had a more measured disposition, would get irritated, hiss at her mom, shut her down, and walk away. It was hard to watch, because her mom had such pure intentions. As we worked together, we learned her daughter felt overwhelmed by her mom's energy. Her mom's pacing frustrated her, but she didn't know why or how to tell her mom, so she got mad and left.

Mom was never going to change to match her daughter's pacing, but she was able to empathize that her energy felt too large to her daughter, and by slightly curbing her excitement and pausing more as she asked her questions, her daughter was able to join her in conversation more. The daughter learned why she was pushing her mom away and that her mom's energy and excitement came from how deeply she cared for her daughter. This also helped her stay in conversation with her mom and tell her when she felt overwhelmed.

- **We can sidestep the Fix-It Syndrome.**
We care so much for our tween that when they are upset, we often move quickly to stop the emotion by dismissing it, erasing the pain, and taking care of them. Ironically, this has just the opposite effect, pushing them across the bridge of the emotional scale into frustration and anger as our move to repair the situation leaves them feeling unheard and frustrated—dysregulated. Note: If your tween starts to rev up at your suggestions, know they are probably moving over the bridge.

It can go like this: Your daughter comes home from school saying her friend group is leaving her out. It is the second time this week this has happened, and you see a "mean girls" situation brewing. Your gut instinct is to call the girls' parents. You know exactly what you would like to say and how you think the situation should go. And you want to tell your daughter…what? Maybe you had a similar experience in middle school, and your own sadness resurfaces, so perhaps you want to shut it all down—spare her the pain you felt—and say to her, "You know what, they aren't good friends, you will find other friends," or "Just ignore it, they don't mean to do that." "Fixing" or dismissing the pain does not honor her and the experience that is upsetting her. Rather, it will leave her feeling unseen and in it alone. In most cases, she will either walk away, shut down, or get mad.

Instead, when our tween is hurting, ask about their experience. Listen. Find out what it feels like for them using what we covered in the emotional awareness section. Next, wonder with them how to handle the situation. Let them think it through; let them lead. Giving our tween space and time to be heard, to use their own voice, can be calming.

Not letting our tweens experience discomfort and work through their emotions or encouraging them to "never mind" something that is upsetting them will create problems later in life. When similar emotions surface, they won't know how to cope with them; they might fear the feelings and be overwhelmed. I see many adults stuck in negative self-talk, or they may shut down or wind up with anger management problems because they did not practice emotional expression when they were young.

Remember, emotional expression and emotional regulation go hand in hand. So, to help our tween manage their emotions, we *can* offer suggestions on how to express them. This is different from giving the answer. It is more of a wondering with them about what could work. We still make them do the thinking.

For example, we all know anger expressed as yelling, name calling, swearing, and throwing things serves no one, least of all our tween, who feels terrible in the wake of these behaviors. Instead, we might suggest, "What if you tried A? Play that out, what might happen? What else might happen? Okay, how would you tweak it a bit? What might happen? Could this other thing happen? If A or B is not quite right, what do you think the next option could be? Do you want to start there?" Remember, the "solve" is around expressing emotion.

It is important to note that if we provide no direction to our tween for how to express their intense feelings, we also leave them alone in their potentially bad choices and the guilt and regret that follow. We don't protect them from themselves. As a result, we become "an unsafe adult" for them: They won't trust us.

- **We can empathize.**

  Conflict with a teacher, disagreements with a friend or teammate, test anxiety, or underperforming in sports—all can be devastating for tweens. We know that. As adults, we also know these problems are peanuts in comparison to the bigger issues we face as life goes on. Still, we must remember this is the first time our tween is experiencing these things, and they often feel unsure, insecure, overwhelmed, or physically ill because of them. We must also keep this in mind when their emotions run hot or they are hard to reach and we find ourselves getting angry, frustrated, or worried about them.

  If we can hold our own reactions, table any concerns about their intense emotions—regardless of how inappropriate or out of proportion they may be—and focus instead on what they are experiencing and what triggered the experience…if we can *really* listen, our tween will feel reassured, secure, and more confident in themselves.

- **We can teach our tween to be mindful.**

  Mindfulness is Eastern medicine's way of regulating emotions. As we covered in Part Four: Remediating Our Soil, it allows the body to honor emotion but let it go, to keep it from taking over, and our tween can learn it too through breathing, paying attention to their immediate surroundings, meditation, and more. With mindfulness, our tween preempts dysregulation, dropping into the here and now with the ability to view their immediate situation with perspective. For example, a mindful tween might think: *I feel embarrassed by those kids at school. I understand that about myself. I know my options are to: 1. Talk to an adult about my feelings or ask for help, 2. Stay away from bullies and stick with good friends, or 3. Have words to keep the mean kids away.* Mindfulness also keeps our tween from obsessing or sinking into a shame spiral (which we definitely don't want our tween's developing brain to get good at).

The Art of the Pivot

I often tell my clients we want to sit in the soil issue to understand it, conquer it. We do *not* want to lie down, roll around, and get all comfy in it. The same goes with our tween. When things are tough and they are in dire need of regulating, sometimes the best thing to do is give them a break from all that's weighing on them—as you might do when they're feeling sad. Send them in another direction—sports, dance, drawing, shopping; make up a game, run around the yard, the park, blast the tunes and dance…anything that allows your tween to separate, to blow off steam. It can stop the shame spiral and help restore their equilibrium, and their openness later to talking about what's on their mind, rather than igniting or shutting down.

CHAPTER TWENTY-THREE

WEATHER REPORT: READING OUR TWEEN

If we are to succeed in helping our tween start to identify, understand, express, and regulate their emotions, we must be able to read them, meet them where they are, then choose the best way to interact with them to keep the path between us clear, to stay regulated ourselves. Different situations will call for different behaviors from us. It's a bit like knowing what to do in a variety of weather conditions. In this case, our tween is the weather and we are the response to it.

The Storm

When rain meets wind, hail, thunder, and lightning, trees bend; things untether and crash. A tree may fall, roads could flood. Who wants to be out in that?! Similarly, when a tween is blowing their top, parents typically skedaddle or tell them to *"STOP IT!"* Emotions are running way too hot (which can very easily become prime time for any lurking soil issues as well, intensifying the storm!).

But the heat has meaning, and if we can separate ourselves from it—get under the wave—and either let our tween know we see it or give them room to cool down (it's often as impossible to stop a tween midstorm as it is to halt a deluge outside…we're better off waiting for the squall to pass), they will sense the space available to be heard, and we will be able to find out what their anger is really all about. For example, we can say, "I see you're really mad and frustrated. Do you want to talk about it, or do you need a little time to yourself?" If they yell something ugly at us, we need not comment, not in that moment, at least. We can come back to it after things cool off.

The Harmattan

If you've been to the Sahara, you may know all about the harmattan. It's a dry, hot wind that blows in the winter months, driving sand and grit into every pore. It usually comes with a haze that obscures the sun, and it's unrelenting. Anxiety is like this. It wears on a tween, stripping them of their energy, layer by layer, while it locks them in place. It's words, words, and more words, and thoughts and emotions but no resolution. Anxious tweens are thinkers and tend to worry about the future. Their anxiety can be sparked by something small such as "I can't find my shoes. We're going to be late for practice!" or a larger issue such as "My friends didn't sit with me today at lunch. What's wrong with me?" Ours is not to judge the source of the anxiety when it has our tween in its grip. Rather, our goal is to help them slow down and regain their calm, because once they have settled down a bit, they will be able to talk through their situation more rationally. It's about returning our tween to the present moment. Here are three of my favorite ways to do this: *Note: These can work for us as well when we are feeling anxious!*

- **Be Sense-able**
  Ask your tween to look around and find five things they can *see*, four things they can *touch*, three things they can *hear*, two things they can *smell*, and one thing they can *taste* (within reason—my son will put anything in his mouth, even as a tween! Last week he drank rainwater out of a tube holding wires. Could that be a neural sprouting misfire?).

- **The Magic Touch**

  Tell your tween to touch the tip of each finger with their thumb. As they do it, ask them to say (quietly or out loud): I (pointer), Can (middle finger), Handle (ring finger), This (pinky). Repeat as needed.

- **Take a Breather**

  In an anxious moment, often our tween may be holding their breath or crying, so this breathing exercise can also work to loosen the hold anxiety has on them. Have your tween take a breath to the count of four, hold it, then slowly release it to the count of eight. This will send oxygen through the bloodstream, which calms the nervous system, as we discussed in Part Six: I See You. (This is one of the reasons why "breath work"—yes, it's a thing—and meditation are so popular.)

When Anxiety Hides: What to Watch For

Some tweens are like ducks: They may appear calm, gliding gracefully across the water, but beneath the surface, their legs are churning, moving like mad to keep going. We have to look even closer here. We may be able to see their anxiety in their facial expressions or if their usual easygoing demeanor gives way to impatience. They may also appear tense. Some tweens express anxiety by being less talkative or through negativity. An anxious tween may also be overly sensitive, blowing up over something that appears benign.

Sunny with a Swirling Breeze

Hyper tweens tend to be like a swirling breeze when the sun is bright: It may be a stunner of a day but it's not quite comfortable; there's a little too much air. These tweens move *fast* with endless energy, but they have a hard time sitting still and even more difficulty concentrating. For many tweens, this is simply their normal state. For others, it is their way of decompressing after sitting in school following a ton of directions for days on end. Typically, this tween is creative and fun-loving. They are more apt to prefer being outside playing sports, riding bikes, or engaged in some other physical fun over quiet indoor activities. They also tend to do better with quick, small tasks rather than those that are more complex and time-consuming.

We can help them find the focus to tackle bigger projects that require more concentration by breaking them into smaller steps. We can also teach them strategies such as taking short, frequent breaks and multitasking (though this tween may also thrive at multitasking). We must observe our tween and see what works for them rather than trying to superimpose what works for us or "most people." This is one of the biggest mistakes I see parents make. We miss the chance to really know our tween and how they tick.

Keep in mind, if this tween is struggling with a problem (the clouds roll in), their hyper-energy can manifest into anxiety or anger and impulsive behavior. Knowing this helps us understand where their emotions may be coming from so that we can respond appropriately.

When It's Cloudy

At the other end of the spectrum is the overcast day. This is our tween when they are feeling sad, disappointed, defeated, and depressed. They have little energy: The cloud feels so heavy. They may retreat into quiet. To see a tween in this place is heartbreaking.

We want to fix it so they feel better, and we think the sooner we can do that, the better. But the more we try to fix whatever is bothering them, the more persistent it becomes. And it seems to last forever—but it doesn't really. As parents, our best course of action is patience. We must sit with them until it passes, let them steer the conversation while we ask questions and work to understand what is bothering them rather than trying to make it pass for them. Perhaps they are feeling compassion for a friend going through something difficult, and that is the source of their sadness. Or maybe life is hard for them at school or with their peers. If a peer problem, after listening to them, we might ask, "Oh, and when they do X, what do you think? How does it make you feel?" or "What could you do when that happens?"

We have to be sure to keep an eye on the frequency of these cloudy days and just how dark they get, factoring in whether or not there is a family history of depression to determine if there is a bigger problem. Certainly if the darkness escalates to cutting, talk of hurting themselves, or comments like, "Life would be better without me in it," find a therapist ASAP.

When Hyper Goes Too Far

Some tweens struggle with hyperactivity and inattentiveness more than is developmentally typical and may exhibit symptoms of Attention Deficit Hyperactivity Disorder (ADHD). These include:

- Impulsive behaviors
- Inability to concentrate
- Trouble with follow-through
- Short attention span, easily distracted
- Difficulty following instructions
- Restless body movement
- Trouble sitting for very long
- Forgetfulness (their memory is not sharp because tweens with ADHD are easily distracted, not because of an actual memory issue)
- Difficulty engaging in quiet or structured activities
- Attitude issues (not because they choose a bad attitude but rather as a result of being inattentive: tweens with ADHD miss social timing)

If you're worried about your tween, absolutely take them to a psychologist or psychiatrist to be assessed.

At Sunset

Every sunset is different, but beautiful too, each in its own way…just like tweens when they are in their happy zone. This is our tween at their most content, shooting their color into their life, like the sky as the sun dips below the horizon. Our tween may look different than we do when we are happy, which sometimes throws us off, prompting criticism (creating rain where there is none). Our tween might be telling us what they consider to be silly jokes or trying to engage us through teasing or pranks. Rather than stopping them or trying to "correct" their behavior, we should remember to:

- park with our tween in their joy.
- marvel at our maturing, changing child.
- take a moment to simply watch and enjoy them.
- stop what we are doing and play or chat…even if it's about nothing in particular.

We can let them decide how to spend time. Give them the lead, to bake, paint a picture, organize their room the way *they* want, or create a big (fill in the blank: fort, obstacle course, collage, whatever) even if it makes a mess and leaves little to show for the time, effort, and materials put into it. Because, in fact, we'll have *a lot* to show for it: Our tween will feel seen, heard, and *known*, with newfound confidence if they've tried something they've never done before.

Oh, That Changeable Weather!
About Those Conflicting Emotions...

The parents of a tween I was working with were going through a divorce. The tween told me he felt excited about his mom's new house and going on ski trips with just his dad, but then he also felt guilty for being happy about the divorce. Certainly conflicting emotions are trickier to untangle, but they too are a normal part of life.

When your tween tells a story, listen for conflicting or opposite feelings. You might say, "I wonder if you feel a little disappointed by X but a little relieved about Y." I've heard tweens who make a less competitive sports team say they feel disappointed they didn't make the best team but also that they are relieved because they were intimidated by the expectations of the more competitive team. The important thing is to normalize this for them; tell them we all often feel conflicting emotions.

The Other Side of Sunny: When to Seek More Help

Just as the weather changes throughout the day and can vary endlessly, so can our tween's moods. Keep in mind, there is a normal spectrum of emotions our tweens will experience, including anger, disappointment, and other hard-to-watch reactions. Tears are normal. Anger and yelling are normal. Fretting is normal. Forgetting, impulsivity, pushing back are all normal. What we want to watch for are behaviors and emotions outside the common scope of tween development, things we covered in Part Two: It's Not You, It's Neuroscience (Tangled Vines) such as:

- The tough emotions appear more frequently.
- You cannot tie the tough emotions to a trigger.
- The tough emotions become our tween's state of being.
- Our tween has a hard time managing their emotions after several attempts.
- Our tween's behaviors become extreme: Tears last for hours or return often; anxiety does not decrease; there's much more backtalk and it is more intense.
- We see self-harming behaviors around food (controlling when and how much they eat), over-exercising, scratching, or cutting.

Looking Ahead

As you will recall from Part Two: It's Not You, It's Neuroscience, our tween is in formation. I keep coming back to this because it is one of the most important takeaways from the book. The pathways in our tween's brain are under development. Those most often used will grow to roads, interstates, superhighways. Those not used will fade to barely discernible footpaths until they eventually disappear in later adolescence, when the brain prunes them away. What remains are the habits and patterns that will shape every aspect of our child's life. So now is the time to drill down and build the emotional intelligence that will sustain them through high school and beyond.

QUESTIONS TO PONDER

1. How comfortable do you feel talking about feelings and emotions? How important do you think it is to understand and talk about feelings? Your answers to these questions will dictate how willing and able you may be to teach your tweens these skills.

2. Most parents want to fix things for their tweens; do you relate to that? If so, what are some things you are trying to fix that you might give to your tween to handle?

3. What behaviors do you see in your tween when their feelings are registering 1 to 3 on the Emotion Scale? 4 to 6? 7 to 10? What things help calm them down?

4. What do you notice are your tween's most common feelings?

PART EIGHT

I Am Here for You

The Glue That Makes Us Strong

"No society in time or place has thrived in isolation."

—AMANDA CRAIG, PHD, LMFT

"And above all these put on love, which binds
everything together in perfect harmony."

—COLOSSIANS 3:14 ESV

s there any more solid foundation for life than the certainty of unconditional belonging, a knowledge that there are people who have our back, no matter what? We know this from our faith communities. Our tween knows it too, though they may not be aware consciously of just how important it is to them. I'm talking about the kind of bond that comes from shared stories, mannerisms, values, traditions; from time together and really knowing one another. They are all expressions of love, another key to emotional connection, and our tween gets it through being part of a church, a community, any group that makes them feel supported and cared for. When it comes from family, it is truly a magic carpet, carrying them through the ups and downs of this crazy growth period. It's a steadfast reminder that they are loved, supported, and good enough just as they are, which gives them courage to try hard things and take healthy risks. They know we're there for them. For us, it is a ticket to our tween, the relationship we long to have with them and the kind of parent we need to be to set the stage for the rest of their lives!

We build family connection through *how we spend time* together. That starts with engaging our tween. Here's how.

CHAPTER TWENTY-FOUR

SPEAK THEIR (LOVE) LANGUAGE

Each of us has our own love language. Coined by Gary Chapman, PhD, author, radio talk show host, and senior associate pastor at Calvary Baptist Church in Winston-Salem, North Carolina, with the publication of the first of his series of books, *The Five Love Languages*, in 1992, our love language shapes how we communicate care and connection. It is what comes most naturally to us. We know our love language by the way we respond to the way others interact with us. We know the love language of others by the way they respond to us. Love language can be verbal or nonverbal—tone of voice or touch. It can be time together, helping solve problems, talking through hurts, positive feedback, or a hug.

We use *our* love language to communicate care to our tween when we are inviting them into the family fold. We tend to give love in the ways we want to receive love. They respond based on *their* love language. The two aren't necessarily the same and can lead to some major disconnects, unintentional as they may be. Here's why: All day long we can affirm our tween, affirm our tween, affirm our tween. We can put a note in with the lunch we lovingly make for them. We can say "Good job!" and put their report card on the refrigerator. But, if time is their love language, all this affirmation won't land.

Maybe our tween's love language is simply being in the same room with us, doing errands with us, hanging with us while we fold laundry, not necessarily even saying much. We might wonder why they don't go out to play, but spending time with us is what matters to them.

Perhaps their love language is having us do things for them like cooking, cleaning, giving them rides to activities, driving them to school, having sleepovers at home rather than at someone else's house, etc. The list can be long. For some kids, this is their way of feeling secure. They know what they need will be there for them when they need it. It's not that they are using us. Rather, it's the place they go for comfort.

Maybe our tween is a hugger, and although they are getting older (and bigger), they still like to cuddle on the couch or have us sit in their room and talk about their day at bedtime. This is *their* love language.

From seeing and hearing our tween, we will get a sense of what resonates as care and security to them. You'll see it when it happens through their gratitude. They will ask for it more often. They will engage with us longer.

Meet Them Where They Are

When our tween is not engaging with the rest of the family, we all feel the disconnection. It creates tension. So how do we get them back into the family fold, to feel that sense of belonging that is key to emotional connection? How do we get them to open up? We can start by meeting them where they are. Here's what I mean:

When my son was ten years old, he went through a stage where he didn't want to sit at the dinner table. He said, "You never talk to me." I remember thinking to myself, *All we do is talk to you!* I thought about all the times we asked, "What did you do in school?" "How did you do on the test?" "Who did you hang out with at recess?" etc. What I realized is none of our questions had anything to do with what *he* wanted to talk about. And when he did start to talk about things he enjoyed such as "I want to show you my new house in Roblox," or "Today at recess I was playing football and this kid stepped on my foot," we would move along to another topic or be done with dinner. We missed the mark! He wanted to share with us; we just didn't see how important his topics were. And so dinnertime was a chore for him rather than a time to connect.

If we're not paying attention to where *our tween* is, but where *we* are, we can ask all the questions in the world and they're going to check out. I work with a family where the mom, dad, and two of their children are very similar get-after-it kind of people. The third child, a tween, is more of a Ferdinand the Bull type, happy on his own, smelling the flowers. It drives the mom insane. At the dinner table, conversation is about *What boxes did you check today? What successes did you have today?* And he's always hijacking the conversation into silliness. He told me in session he doesn't relate to his family's conversation. He said, "I feel left out. It doesn't make sense to me. It's always about these things that aren't interesting to me. I don't like that."

Tweens will talk if it's fun, interesting, or about them in a nonjudgmental way. (Note: If you get stuck, in silence, try provocative questions. Tweens tend to *love* these.) While it can be work for us to find the right Q and A to get our tween to open up, it is worth the effort. Because when we do, we learn about them, they learn about us—we connect.

At times, however, meeting our tween where they are has nothing to do with talking. Recently, I was getting ready for work. My five-year-old daughter, Livvy, was a few feet away playing Legos. My tween son, Owen, was two feet away doing a puzzle. There was no question asking, but we were in such a calm space. Nobody was fighting. I could hear Livvy's little voice talking among her Legos. Owen would spew out loud, not really speaking to anyone in particular, "Where's that piece? Oh! Here it is. This is awesome. Look, I got the border." We were in the fold.

Talking to Your Tween

Conversation Starters	To Keep the Conversation Going	If You Get Stuck: Provocative Questions
I notice today you came home with less pep in your step. Did something happen at school?	What was it like in homeroom today? Did you have pizza for lunch? Did you nail that math test?	• Were those same kids off the rails? • Any boys talk to you today? • Any girls talk to you today?
What did you think about: • a social trend? • a favorite sports team who won or lost a recent game? • a current event (pick one)? • that YouTuber?	Oh, interesting. So you think... (paraphrase).	• What did your friends say about it? • Would you ever try that? • When would you use that strategy? • What would you do if you were in his/her shoes?
Did you notice when X happened?	• Tell me if I understand you. You're saying (paraphrase). • What did you think? What would you say or do in that position? Were your friends talking about it?	• Use biologically correct words (e.g., penis, puberty). • Use direct quotes even if there is bad language or swearing.
How did that situation with Y go?	Do you think (this) or (that)?	What if...
Did you play football at lunch?	What happened next?	"Correct me if I'm wrong" statements that are intentionally wrong. (Tweens love to correct parents)
What did your friends say about (current event)?	Do you agree with them? What would you have done?	Would you ever ...? (take an extreme position)
If you could...	Are you saying you'd do A before B?	What would you imagine me doing?
How did (their favorite thing) go?	What was the best part? Where did you get tripped up? Do you think you can do it again next time?	Did you know you... (insert fact about the scenario)?

CHAPTER TWENTY-FIVE

FAMILY FUN, PLAY, AND LAUGHTER

Sometimes we need to stop talking and just have fun...to feel the lightness, calm, and joy, to open our minds and be fully in the moment.

Fun, laughter, and play are the source of some of our most enduring family memories, and no wonder: They bring us together, effortlessly, and they are not only good for family connection, they are good for the mind, body, and soul. When we're happy, we release dopamine, which makes us more alert, focused, and motivated. Fun, laughter, and play make us feel better about life and ourselves. And they're contagious: When someone is laughing, it is nearly impossible for that funny not to bite us too.

The trick is to find the fun in everyday moments—during breakfast, while making lunches if that's part of your routine, after school, at bedtime, and even on vacation. (Just because you are away on a "special" trip is no guarantee of fun. Rather, it's the approach we bring to it and one another. The heart matters more than the stuff.)

But as we get older, this is easier said than done. I hear it all the time from my clients who are in their thirties and forties: They wonder why they can't find fun. I think back to my own childhood, and even to my twenties: It was *all* about fun then, even as I worked toward my PhD. I look at myself now—I'm often exhausted. Fun?! Are you kidding me? Who has the energy for that?!

Bills, work, chores, errands, concern about our kids, never-ending to-do lists. So much for fun, laughter, and play. If we're not careful, these adult priorities can shove fun from the list entirely—despite its many health benefits and what it can do to build emotional connection and cement our relationship with our tween.

A Note on Teasing

To prank each other or direct an ironic or comical remark at a family member can be fun if we have that sense of humor. For example, my son turns on every light in every room he enters in our house. He then leaves them on, so we call him One Way: "Hey! Looks like One Way was in the basement." or "Hey, One Way, did you go through the upstairs?" He knows he does it and smiles with us about how he forgets and that we notice. Also, as a family, we always seem to have one dollop of something left—a tad of ketchup in the bottle or a last swig of milk…just enough for a mouse. Whoever catches it will call out "A mouse is in the house," teasing us all for this goofy thing. We all smile, though we know "mouse in the house" was originally aimed at my husband. He buys in small portions and always leaves the last bite. It became fun because he is not sensitive about it. Like my son with the lights, he knows he does it and that our teasing is a love thing.

However, we have to watch how our kids respond to teasing. Some tweens are more sensitive and will find no humor in it. In fact, it will make them sad. Teasing can also be a slippery slope where one parent joins with the kids to pick on the other parent. When we gang up on one another, emotional connection goes out with the trash.

We can't let this happen. It's not hard. In fact, not being fun is harder because as humans, we naturally want joy. Moments of fun can be quick and peppered throughout the day through music—dancing around the kitchen, cranking the tunes, and singing loudly. Or gentle roughhousing, an inside joke, a spur-of-the-moment ice cream cone, or a quick adventure.

Maybe a walk, hike, bike ride or swim, or something our tween chooses, changing a routine or breaking a rule as a special-occasion kind of thing (why not a picnic dinner on the playroom floor in the middle of winter, just for the fun of it?). You'll find the ideas are endless, and the effort to shelve the responsibilities of adulthood, even if for just a few minutes at a time, well worth the effort. Families who play together stay together. For. Sure.

The Ice Cream Principle

We all need a break sometimes, our tween included! We know this, but we don't always act on it. So many of the parents I see forget this when it comes to their children, and it blows my mind. Take, for example, school: Our tween goes to school six, seven hours a day. Often they go to sports or some extracurricular activity after that. When they come home, we send them straight to homework—no screens, no lollygagging. It's a lot! They're not robots. They need to hit the off switch sometimes, and that's okay. It need not be right after school. When the break comes will be different for every family, and it builds emotional connection. I think of it as the ice cream principle: those serendipitous times when we peel off from our regular routine for an ice cream, when our tween may least expect it, or a bike ride, or to explore a local stream—anything that provides a breather, a departure from routine and rules.

What do you do as a family for fun? Can you come up with three things you envision as family fun and three things your tween envisions as family fun? Keep in mind, your idea of fun and your tween's might be different. If you are not sure what your tween thinks is fun, ask them. Be specific. For example, rather than shoot hoops, think go outside on a cool fall day and play PIG with the basketball. How often do you let your tween pick an activity? Do you go along with their choice even if you don't like it? How often do you sit and watch them or actually play with them during their screen time? There may be many more ways than we've covered here to add fun, play, and laughter to your family life.

The Nature of Fun

Looking for some family glue? Take it outside. Easy hikes through nature preserves, being on or near the water, watching the stars at night, gardening, or simply walking the neighborhood are among the best ways I know to bring family together, to create the kind of belonging we aim for with our tween. Even if you're not an "outdoor family" or your tween grumbles about it, odds are they will remember it as a good experience, part of your family lore. It is hard to be in fresh air and not have lasting, happy impressions. Help your tween notice plants, flowers, animals, insects, and birds. Marvel in discovery. My kids couldn't be more excited when we see fireflies on an evening walk, and how about those deer? Never gets old. Or the wait for a fish to bite and the euphoria when it does! Other benefits of being outside include:

- Exposure to nature is shown to reduce stress and increase attention span.
- When tweens are out in nature, all of their senses are activated.
- Tweens who experience nature are less afraid and more confident around animals. They are more curious about forests, lakes, birds, insects, snakes, and other living things.
- Tweens practice being inquisitive and open in nature. This builds these mental muscles and transfers to other settings.
- Tweens gain an appreciation for the environment. Show a tween who has spent time in nature a picture of a sea turtle wrapped in a plastic straw and see what they do the next time they are offered a straw!

Playing the Field

Sports are among the biggest ways families bond—playing, teaching, coaching, watching, cheering on our child, helping them prepare for a game, a match, a practice. Anyone with a modicum of enthusiasm for any sport knows this. What a blast they can be and what opportunity they hold to teach our children a whole range of life's lessons—from discipline and humility to sportsmanship, teamwork, and more! However, before we launch into sports with our child, and even as we pursue sports with them, we must be sure we are following *their* interests, *their* lead, and not projecting *our* ambitions and wishes on them. We should support them wherever they are, whatever their goals may be, and keep it all in perspective. Whether they are the superstar or a benchwarmer, we must resist the urge to make too big a deal out of it. Consistent, warm, open encouragement will win the day. If sports are not their thing, honor it, as difficult as that may be for parents who are athletes.

CHAPTER TWENTY-SIX

MANTRAS, RITUALS, AND MORE

Mantras connect us in ways unique to us, reminding us we belong. They help show our tween our support for them in all they do. Mantras are phrases, quotes, and one-liners, handshakes, sayings of inspiration or encouragement. They are shortcuts to deeper meaning known only by the people who share them, a mutual understanding triggering memories of shared experiences. They reinforce a common bond. Is there a line you often use with your kids or that your kids often use? It could be a word, a phrase, a look, or even a hand signal. What are one or two short mantras relevant to your family? What is the story the message communicates?

Tweens are notorious for one-liners because they do not screen themselves as much as they will when they are teenagers. So what they say can often have a curious thought behind it. My son said to me one day, "Stop life rushing me!" He felt rushed and overwhelmed and just said it, not thought out and not really out of anger, he just expressed himself. And it stuck. As a family, we now all say "Stop life rushing me!" when we are moving too fast and it's overwhelming or provoking anxiety.

Most recently we are talking about the difficult balancing act between screen time and homework time. We discussed how getting off the screen to do homework or picking up a book and reading before screen time is hard, not fun, and provokes irritation. But when we do our work first, we feel better about relaxing and having fun. We don't have to feel guilt or something looming over our head. We talked about *doing hard things*: Get the important stuff out of the way and then play. *Do hard things.* So now when our son is frustrated by a have-to, we recognize this is an example of doing hard things—and it pays off. And when it was my turn to take out the dog and I tried to get my five-year-old to do it, my son said, "Do hard things." I smiled. I got it.

Family mantras build connection—emotional connection.

Create Rituals

Rituals, like mantras, mark us as unique and give us a story about who we are as a family, connecting us with the common denominator they give us. Rituals can be little things we do daily, weekly, monthly, or once a year on holidays, birthdays, or at the end of the school year. They are grand gestures and simple traditions—anything we do repeatedly as a family or as members of a family. Rituals can be for the whole family, between mother and daughter, mother and son, father and daughter, father and son, or even between siblings. Examples include:

- Pancakes on Saturday mornings
- A girls' afternoon out
- Weekly religious services
- A milkshake after a hard practice
- An early morning run
- Sunday breakfast at a local diner
- Picking the meal on your birthday
- A favorite restaurant
- A song you all sing
- A family grace at meals
- A game you play or a show you watch together
- Family meetings
- A favorite book
- Volunteer work
- Taking turns sharing each day's best part/worst part over dinner

- Hanging specific decorations
- Favorite dishes
- Family hikes or walks around the neighborhood
- Speaking a second language
- Sports you do together as a family
- Playing musical instruments
- Memorizing poetry
- A long hug at night before bed
- Hanging in your tween's room while they clean it (rather than barking the order from another room and hoping it gets done)
- Spending the last twenty minutes of your tween's day doing whatever they choose.

With rituals, pretty much anything is fair game, as long as it fits for your family. Rituals often include homage to past generations and our cultural heritage, further connecting us to all that makes us family—committed to one another and our tween.

What are the things you and your family do together?

Food for Thought

I highly recommend families share a meal together at a table at least once a day. At mealtime, the agenda is set: We are there to eat. There is no baggage, no ulterior motive (most of the time). The expectations are set in our favor to connect. It is a time to talk about things important to us, hear our tweens and what is important to them, look at one another, make eye contact, smile, find joy in conversation. It is a time to reinforce family values, and it ultimately adds to the protective factor we create for our tween: When they know who they are, where they come from, and that they belong to people who listen to them and honor who they are, they are better prepared to resist the pull of negative behaviors during their teen years and beyond.

About Siblings: The Only Friendship We Are Given

This relationship has so much potential to create belonging! It is the sole "friendship" we are given, and it is in our life forever. These are the only people who share family heritage, a childhood experience, and a mom and dad. As their parents, we have such an opportunity to cultivate a relationship between our children that will give them a lifetime of emotional connection. That means letting them play, fight, rough and tumble, figure it out, collaborate, teach each other, and show affection.

Playing and fighting might happen at the same time. Play often leads to fighting. With friends, tweens are so concerned with looking cool, they will hold back. The sibling relationship is where they can let loose, be themselves, and practice skills with someone closer to their age than parents. That is why it is important for parents *not* to fix things for them or keep them apart in order to maintain quiet and peace in the family. We want to encourage siblings to work out their problems and find ways to mend the relationship. It is easy for us to get in the middle, side with younger or less advantaged siblings. Resist this: It only causes potential resentment between siblings and puts a wedge in our relationship with our tween. *Caveat: When there is a safety issue, don't just step in, barge!*

Set Family Goals

The key to using family goal setting to help our tween feel like they really belong is to make the goal attainable, relevant to our kids, and not something that feels like a punishment. If it's *your* goal to get in shape and you set running once a week together as a family goal, make sure it's something your tween wants to do as well. We need their buy-in. Start small, perhaps with something fun such as walking once a week after dinner or making Saturday morning breakfast. Maybe you work to plan a family trip together—it could be a day trip to somewhere local or an adventure farther away. The main thing is to work on it together. Really include your tween.

If it feels like the goal is slipping away, regroup with the family to slice it thinner.

Animal Attraction

We decided during COVID to add ten chickens and a dog to our family. We already had two cats. I thought, *Why not?* I knew animals can bring a family closer—with the shared responsibility, how entertaining they can be, and their unconditional love (with dogs at least. Chickens? Not so much). The benefits have far exceeded my expectations. Have they brought us closer? Certainly, but my son has grown too. Before, he really wasn't an animal person and actually felt kind of cautious around them. He learned responsibility as he cared for them and grew more confident and comfortable with them as he did. He now walks our dog, loves on her. He has met the neighborhood dogs and their owners. He has learned about different breeds and has much more interest in animals in general. He even picks up the chickens without reservation. His world is bigger with things that have expanded the man he will one day become. And there is no end to the bonding hoot it is for our entire family to own this menagerie.

The Power of Culture

We give our tween their best shot at finding the best in themselves when we give them a solid base from which to launch into all areas of their lives. We can do this by helping them know where they come from, regardless of whether they are new to where we live or the latest in a long generational line. In teaching our tween their heritage and customs, we build confidence and belonging. It's not about separating them from their peers but rather providing assurance and security in who they are, so that they understand and embrace their differentiating attributes as a source of strength. It's from there they develop the ability to seek their spot in the world, and the comfort within themselves to see where we all intersect as human beings amidst all that makes us unique.

Do Tough Things Together

Broadcasters have built an empire showcasing people doing hard things together. Whether they are running through obstacle courses or lost in the desert and have to find their way out, people working together to do hard things build character and develop new skill sets. It's the same for families. What difficult things do you tackle as a family? It could be do-it-yourself projects, camping, woodworking, cooking a holiday meal, completing a chore that takes time, muscle, and thought…anything that is challenging. When we do difficult things together, we grow together, we create memories, and we reinforce our ties to each other.

The Art of the Apology

There is definitely an art to saying "I'm sorry." Apologizing is hard. We know that. It's hard because we are unsure if it will land as we intend, unsure of the response we will get, unsure if it will be thrown back at us at some point. Our uncertainties make us vulnerable. It can be hard as well if we come from a family that never apologized or if we think apologizing will convey weakness, especially to our tween. We may think it will affect their trust in us and our ability to protect them.

In reality, apologizing actually brings us closer. It repairs connections and *restores* trust. *Everyone* feels guilt, regret, or disappointment over something done (or left undone!). When we take time to reflect and dig into what drove us to act as we did, or *not* act as we'd wished, we can own our part and find the peace and relief that come with it. What's more, an apology says *I see what I did. I see that it hurt your feelings, and I assure you I will be mindful next time.* This is money for our tweens. It offers hope that future interactions will change and reopens the door to the belonging that is so key to emotional connection.

When we hurt our kids, they feel sad. When we apologize, we validate their feelings and empower our tween to trust those feelings. In contrast, if we say, "If you hadn't done X, I wouldn't have done Y," we are telling them what we did was *their* fault. It is most likely a subconscious way to dodge apologizing—or maybe we don't even realize we're doing it. Either way, it confuses our tween, making them feel insecure, as if they are the reason we act badly, and it separates us. For instance, if our tween asks and asks for that new outfit and we keep saying "No!" until we finally lose our temper then blame them for our outburst in an *If you wouldn't have asked me so many times, I wouldn't have gotten mad* kind of way, we've triggered a breach. It's not because of them. It's because we were unaware in the moment and did not act with intention. We reacted out of anger and frustration—rarely our best look as parents. We should try to avoid escalating to a place where an apology is called for; we can shut down the conversation before it gets to that point saying something like, "I know you really want that but we can't do that today. We can revisit it the end of the week." Or "We already talked about that and we have to move on. What do you want for dinner?" Or "I see you're having trouble accepting a 'no.' Do you want to take a few minutes to yourself? No? Okay, well I'm going to take a few minutes to myself and then I will come back."

Our tween needs to feel our apology so that they learn what it is like to feel bad about how they acted and repair it through an apology of their own. When they do something that is hurtful to another person and they pair it with empathy or guilt, they learn new behaviors. They change. Their brain will hang on to that! If they do not, they will not experience the lessons that accompany sincere apology, which will hurt their relationships over the long term (and not only with us).

Connecting through Prayer

If you have a faith tradition, one of the most powerful ways families can feel connected and boldly stand together is through prayer. Families that pray together align their values. When they feel depleted and need help, they communicate, as one voice, what they are grateful for. They ask for forgiveness when they make mistakes and lift up those who are suffering in their community and around the world, which builds empathy.

The practice of prayer can be a powerful experience for tweens as parents model how to stand by family values and beliefs and sit in humility. The humility comes from being vulnerable, open, and authentic to one's true self. It shows our tween it is important to be honest about our fears and trust that there is strength beyond ourselves to handle our challenges.

Through prayer, we also give our children a chance to practice pulling from inside themselves to talk about things that may be weighing on them, without any correction or direction. When they are heard in their humility by parents and accepted, they build confidence to be honest and open. They will take time to be more real about what they feel and think and put words to it, because they know it will be seen and accepted by those most important to them.

We can pray at meals, at bedtime, when things are difficult, and when we recognize our blessings. We can pray formally and/or informally—quick petitions as an ambulance goes by for the person inside or at drop-off to a game that everyone stay safe and practice good team spirit.

Making It Stick

Of all the tools available to us to build emotional connection with our tween, these "glue sticks," as I think of them, that reinforce belonging and tell our tween *I am here for you* unconditionally are among my favorite. They are such a reflection of what is modeled for us in our faith communities. And also, who *wouldn't* want an ice cream cone at some serendipitous moment?! But none of it works without boundaries. They're up next.

QUESTIONS TO PONDER

1. What are ways you play, laugh, and find joy as a family?

2. Do you have family traditions?

3. Is there something you always say that is unique to your family?

4. What are three things you can do to create more family bonding?

5. What might you do to teach your tween more about their ethnic and cultural heritage?

PART NINE

I Will Keep You Safe

When It's Time to Drop the Hammer

"Throughout the U.S., it has become cool for children and teens
to disrespect parents and adults generally…the culture of disrespect
mingles with the culture of 'Live for Now.' It is the default culture
which American kids encounter if we set them loose to navigate
without adult direction. Without authoritative guidance,
it is the culture which they will adopt as their own."

—LEONARD SAX, MD, PHD, PHYSICIAN, PSYCHOLOGIST, AUTHOR

"There is no fear in love. But perfect love drives out fear,
because fear has to do with punishment.
The one who fears is not made perfect in love."

—1 JOHN 4:18 NIV

Now, about those boundaries: They are among the most common reasons parents of tweens find their way to me. Their tween isn't following the rules, and there is a ton of conflict in the family. By the time they get to my office, negative feedback loops are in full swing and wreaking havoc on empathy parents might have for their tween. Trust is broken. They are unable to "see" their tween, who is guarded and suspicious of anything their parents say.

That's why I start with how we must actively listen, show we care, that is, *connect emotionally*. This always surprises parents. Ironically, if we neglect the bond with our tween and focus only on boundaries, we'll never be able to effectively set and enforce them…not with any semblance of peace. (As you may recall from the opening chapter: *Hard conversations demand relationship*. This bears repeating…and repeating…and repeating!)

As you also know from earlier chapters, when we actively listen to our tween, we show we are open to what they have to say. This builds their confidence, assertiveness, and wisdom. We teach emotional intelligence, which paves the way to good coping skills and empathy toward others. And when we offer a family that makes them feel cared for and part of something bigger than themselves—a place where they truly belong—they develop an internal sense of being loved and good enough as they are. It is a mirror of what we receive from our faith, from God. It helps them be open to taking healthy risks, trying things that are difficult: They will bounce back if what they attempt doesn't work out. They know we have their back. We have an emotional connection with them. They trust us. And *this* is where boundaries come in.

Note: If you are at the point where your tween feels out of control and you have drifted so far apart, revisit the previous Toolbox chapters, starting with Part Six: I See You, and practice the relationship-building strategies we covered. Once you re-establish solid, positive feedback loops, you can start to implement more boundaries. If you think you are beyond connecting and worry that there may be a mental health issue with your tween, please return to Part Two: It's Not You, It's Neuroscience and review the information in the Tangled Vines section.

Boundaries are acts of love. Certainly we want to give our tween the same kind of space to grow, make choices, and learn from mistakes that we receive from God through our faith. But we must set a perimeter for them, as God does for us, a way to pull them back when they are veering in dangerous or unhealthy directions. With boundaries, our tween feels protected, in the moment and in the long run, even though they may not realize this when we are enforcing them. Boundaries give our tween the chance to feel discomfort, boredom, disappointment, guilt, regret, and unhappiness. Our tween learns they cannot always get their way. Boundaries teach tweens to follow directions (even if they don't like them) and give them the opportunity to experience patience and delayed gratification, to practice doing hard things such as missing messages on a text string that come in after their electronic curfew, being the last kid to get a phone, or explaining to friends why they are not allowed to go to town unsupervised. In setting and enforcing boundaries, we are helping our tween work toward internalizing all this so that they can apply it to their future life choices and relationships. A tween who learns boundaries makes better decisions and becomes a resilient, self-reliant, directed adult able to transition between work and play more successfully. As my tween son said to me one day, "You have to scold me to help me live."

CHAPTER TWENTY-SEVEN

BOUNDARIES AND CONSEQUENCES

To effectively set boundaries with our tween, we must understand how boundaries differ from rules. Rules are rigid and narrow with no room for natural consequences. We set rules to *control* our tween's behavior. Rules often involve badgering and lead to punishment, power struggles, and tempers. When rules are broken, we can feel taken advantage of and our tween can feel ashamed and bad, which breaks our parent–tween connection. Rules can be impulsive and tend to have a negative tone. They are often barked in the heat of a moment rather than thoughtfully executed. Typically, tweens will follow rules because they fear the punishment. Rules fixate more on a specific behavior and don't factor in our relationship with our tween or building life skills.

Boundaries have bigger meaning. They are a teaching tool and build important life skills such as delayed gratification, self-discipline, etc. They give us space to talk about the behavior we aim to instill and why it matters. They are about our relationship with our tween. They don't work without engagement. They are proactive and not so much about changing one behavior as reinforcing our overall value system. Boundaries help our tween develop a moral compass, one that leads to a lifestyle that supports mental, physical, and spiritual wellness. With boundaries, our tween learns to own their behavior. Boundaries allow room for them to experience the natural consequences of their choices: With boundaries, we give our tween a length of rope to trip on, a chance to practice exercising their free will.

Boundaries require parenting…just maybe not always the kind you think. For example, all parents want their kids off screens, but they tend to demand it based on a rule, with no engagement. It's like this: If I say to my son, "Get off that screen. You're at your limit for today. Go find something else to do," he'll say, "Uh, no thanks," and we will argue. If I say, "Hey, you're at your screen time max for today. Let's go run some errands or walk the dog. I want to hear what you think about X. Come with me," I'm communicating there are more productive things for him to engage in than endless screen time, that I want time with him, it's a priority, and that means screens off for now. That's a boundary.

While boundaries are driven by parental wisdom, they do factor in our tween's needs, preferences, and dignity. For example, in deciding when to allow our tween to have a cell phone, we can set rules as a prerequisite. We might say, "If you want a cell phone, you must make your bed, brush your teeth, and do your homework and three chores every day." We remind our tween each time they break one of the rules, which quickly turns to nagging and can become exhausting within days.

Or we can establish boundaries.

As I explain this to the parents in my practice, they inevitably ask me, "So I'm supposed to just let my tween do what they want and smile at them, be calm and understanding like it's all okay?" No! There are limits to behaviors we will tolerate and times when we *must* drop the hammer. Here's how it works:

With a boundary, we tell our tween we understand it is developmentally appropriate for them to want a phone. We communicate that we want them to have one, to fit in with their peers and experience the benefits of the growing independence it represents. However, a phone can be a distraction, and before allowing them to have one, we need to know they can be responsible in other areas of their life such as brushing their teeth, making their bed, completing their homework, and doing their chores. We set the stage for them to "earn" the phone with the choices they make. We establish a time to review their progress, for example when they get their semester grades, and talk about it in the interim in the context of how they are coming along in developing the habits needed to demonstrate to us the responsibility necessary to handle a phone. We need not point out when they don't follow through. We allow space for natural consequences (more on this below).

Boundaries and Rules: How They Differ

Rule	Boundary
You have reached the limit of your time on the computer. Shut it off!	I will give you time to finish this segment of the game you're playing, then you have to shut it down.
You are not allowed to go downtown by yourself.	You have to go downtown with an adult or let me know who you are with, where you are going, and when you will be home.
Your bedtime is nine p.m.	Room time starts at eight-thirty p.m. Lights out at nine p.m. If you stay up later, you will be tired tomorrow, and that will make the school day more difficult.
You get two hours of screen time on Saturday and Sunday.	You get two hours of screen time on Saturdays and Sundays. More than that cuts into family time and other things that are better for your brain. If you go over, I will have to shut down the screens for the next day.
No uploading videos to TikTok unless they are parent-approved.	I need to look at your TikTok videos with you before you post them. That way, we can make sure you are safe and uploading interesting, fun things that are not negative or hurtful to others.
No YouTube viewing without an adult.	Until you are older, I want to see what you are watching on YouTube. I'm curious about what interests you, but there are also a lot of things that are not meant for your age, and I want to make sure you aren't finding those, or if you do, we're together to talk about what they are.

Boundaries and Rules: How They Differ

Rule	Boundary
No video games with guns.	When your brain is more developed, you can play video games with guns, but for now you really need to stick to video games that are sports-oriented, etc. We don't think your mind needs to be strategizing fighting and shooting just yet.
You *must* devote thirty minutes a day (minimum) to homework and/or reading.	I want you to develop good study habits, and the best way to do that is practice. That means at least a half hour of studying and/or reading a day. When you get a little older, schoolwork will become harder and you will be glad you developed a solid homework routine. If you don't, you may get overwhelmed by school.
No dessert if you don't eat your vegetables.	A well-balanced diet should include healthy food *and* fun food. Too much of a bad thing such as sugar makes healthy food not taste as good. You'll be less open to trying new things and eating things that will help your brain and body work best. So, if you want dessert, you have to eat your vegetables first.
You must do three chores before you are allowed to hang.	Part of being a member of this family is chores. When everyone does their share, it makes things easier on everyone, so chores come before fun time. I appreciate the time and effort you put into helping.

Setting Boundaries

Begin with just one or two boundaries. If we set too many boundaries, we will find ourselves on the defense, "raging," as my tween would say, and correcting behavior "all the time." This can leave us feeling depleted, used, and facing an even more rebellious tween. Remember, if and when we ever do concede a boundary, a tween will often double down to fight our system even harder, because they learn if they try hard enough, they will eventually get their way. *Read that sentence again: It is one of the most common things I see parents do, even though it makes our job of parenting so much harder than it needs to be.* So, yes, start with just a couple boundaries and follow this road map.

Be Clear about Why You Are Setting a Boundary

Before you set a boundary, think it through. Be sure you have a good sense of what you are trying to accomplish. Is the boundary:

- A prevention measure for a behavior you don't want your tween to experiment with?
- An intervention for an inappropriate behavior your tween has started to exhibit?
- An opportunity for your tween to practice independence through a previously off-limits activity such as going to town with friends, a sleepover, walking home from school, or owning a cell phone?

Establish Consequences

The first thing to keep in mind as you look to establish consequences for broken boundaries is this: Consequences are not punishments. As boundaries are to rules, consequences are to punishments.

A punishment enforces compliance but does not deliver a message or instill a value system. Punishment is controlling and often includes put-downs, character assassinations, outsmarting tactics, spanking, yelling, or shaming in front of others. A punishment is often delivered in anger, and is frequently reactive rather than preplanned and discussed. Generally, punishments attach to character rather than the transgression, which can leave our tween feeling they are bad, wrong, or unimportant. (The message they receive is *they* are bad rather than *what they did* was bad. As our faith teachings tell us: "Hate the sin, not the sinner.") Punishments can be humiliating and make a tween feel defeated, hurt, and/or mad. Over time, the humiliation our tween may feel and the power we claim with our punishments may lead them to question their self-worth and strip them of their confidence. When the punishment provokes anger, our tween will focus on their fury toward us rather than the behavior we want them to change.

Consequences deliver a message and reinforce a value system. Our tween learns from consequences. For the best results, keep consequences

Truth in Consequences:
How They Are Different from Punishments

Broken Boundary	Punishment	Consequence
Tween is bullying through social media or posting rude, foul, or lewd language.	Social media shame them—posting pictures or stories that embarrass the tween.	Remove the app until they are older, after they learn it is not intended to be used for the content they are posting.
Tween loses their temper and says mean, hurtful things.	Embarrass them by calling them out in front of others.	Discuss their behavior when both parent and tween are calm. Offer tween space to share their perspective.
Tween throws the game controller.	Threaten to take away or hide the controller.	Remove the controller for a period of time because they are not treating it with respect. If they break it, don't replace it, or have them earn the money to replace it themselves.
Tween is not completing chores after being reminded.	Yell put-downs such as "You are so lazy!" or "What is wrong with you?!"	As a regular course of action, withhold screens or other privileges until the chores are completed.
Tween isn't completing schoolwork.	Demand they stay in their room without coming out until their assignments are complete.	Sit down with them to review assignments, look at where they are struggling, and coach them on how to ask their teachers for help.
Tween is caught in a lie.	Refuse to talk to them/withhold love.	Have a conversation about lying, invite them to correct the lie, and brainstorm ways they can do that.

short, immediate, and in line with the boundary violated. One of the biggest potholes I see parents fall into is blurting out a consequence so unreasonable, it is hard to enforce and robs us of consequences for other breaches. For instance, a boundary is violated and we take away screens for a week. The next boundary is violated, now what? Furthermore, we've just set ourselves up for a week of negotiating every time our tween wants screen time. *Better:* Take away screens for the rest of the day. We make our point just as effectively. Unless the violation truly warrants a greater consequence, we don't get much value added with the longer time.

Last, set consequences that relate to the boundary violated. I've heard things such as:

> *"You didn't do your homework, so you can't go to football practice."*
> *"You didn't get off the screen, so you can't have dessert."*
> *"You lied to us about where you were, so you've lost screen time for*
> *a week."*

This is like doing squats to tone your arm muscles. There's no connection, so it's harder for our tween to code the lesson in their mind. Here are examples of consequences that pair well with the boundary violated and intended lesson.

The Broken Boundary: *"You went over your screen time."*
Consequence: *"No screens the rest of the day to let your brain rest and give your body some exercise."*

The Broken Boundary: *"We notice on social media you're swearing and making lewd comments."*
Consequence: *"We'd like to see your content before you post. If you don't show us your content, we will have to shut down that app until you are older."*

Natural Consequences: A Parent's Best Friend

Natural consequences are a parent's best friend. They are affirmations of the boundaries we set and ask very little of us. They come from us but also from teachers, peers, and anyone with whom our tween interacts. We need merely step aside and let them work their magic. That's not always so easy to do: With decades of wisdom, parents can often see trouble coming a

Paying the Price: Natural Consequences

Boundary Breached	Natural Consequence
We ask our tween to brush their teeth. They skip it.	Their breath smells and their peers tell them. They get a cavity and it hurts to get it filled.
Our tween refuses to bathe/use deodorant.	Friends tease them because they're stinky.
Our tween insists on wearing provocative clothing.	They get unwanted peer attention and judgment.
Our tween knows we want them to complete their homework. They ignore us.	Grades drop, and tween is embarrassed when peers share the grades they get after studying.
Our tween refuses to eat at mealtime and because of between-meal snacking on sugar.	Hunger, when we offer food only at mealtime and buy only very limited quantities of sugary snacks so they run out quickly, long before the next grocery shop.
We tell our tween to plug in their screen. They don't.	Screen runs out of battery.
We ask our tween to take out the dog while it's sunny. They procrastinate.	They wind up having to walk the dog when it's raining, dark, and a much bigger task than it would have been had they gone earlier.
Our tween uses their allotted screen time in the morning.	They have no screen time left when a friend comes over later in the day.
Our tween stays up way past nine p.m. lights out.	They are tired and rushed in the morning, grouchy toward the family, and school feels so much harder.

mile away, and we either stop it before it becomes a problem or we resolve the issue with the least amount of pain. When we do this for our tween, we rob them of valuable chances to learn from the natural consequences of their actions (or inaction) and, inadvertently, we teach them helplessness. Sparing ourselves (and our tween) pain in the short term guarantees them difficulties as they get older.

When we allow our tween to make a mistake and experience the natural consequences of it, their brain processes and records it for future reference. They learn how it feels to goof up, goof off, and disobey us—in things big and small. They feel the discomfort and ramifications of their choices. They understand that delay can make simple tasks more difficult. They learn to make different decisions, and they learn to recover from their errors. They develop resilience, resourcefulness, and accountability—for the present and future, in high school, college, and beyond, when there is more on the line.

The best boundaries place an onus on our tween to follow them. When we empower them to make a choice, we give them ownership of the outcome. This works really well with natural consequences, when we let go of the fight and let the outcome speak for us. We're still saying, "It's nine p.m., you have to go to bed." But we let our tween decide when to turn off the lights. If they choose to stay up late, we let them feel tired, cranky, and unhappy at school the next day. Here's how natural consequences worked for a recent client.

A parent was in my office talking about how exhausted she was constantly telling her seventh grade son to study. Each night she'd repeatedly say, "Do your homework," then argue with him when he refused, particularly if she saw him "wasting time playing games on the computer."

She wanted him to work to his potential. She excused her interference because she was paying a high tuition for his private school and knew he had untapped capabilities. Both mother and son were frustrated, and neither felt like talking or spending time together.

The mother and I discussed a way to work through the homework problem—to make her son understand his responsibilities, while allowing him to make his own decisions about handling school assignments. Here's what happened:

- Mom set her expectations: Prepare daily for class and tests, study at night, and limit screen time to one hour per day.
- She promised to remind her son about his homework once a day, no more.
- Initially, her son took advantage of the new rules. He did not use electronic media, but he did watch television and generally wasted time. She kept to her part of the bargain.
- As her son's grades and team assignments began to reflect his choices, his mother found he began to understand his responsibility for homework and meeting goals.
- He began completing his assignments and received much better grades on tests. In addition, in classes where his performance was poor, he felt guilty and started talking about how to improve.

What to Do When the Stakes Are Too High for Natural Consequences

The stakes are rarely too high during the tween years to forego natural consequences. That happens later, during the teen years and beyond, when partying and the potential for promiscuity hit their lives, when the ramifications of bad choices are more serious. It is much easier to allow our tween to bomb a test after choosing to play video games over studying than it is to stand by when they are a junior in high school preparing to apply to college and make a similar goof. So we must learn to tolerate the discomfort we feel when we let our tween fail. Saving them in the short run can submarine them down the road.

Of course there were still times when he didn't do well on tests. But he discussed his performance with his mother, sharing how the low grade affected him, why he did not want to experience the results again, and what he could do differently in the future. The guilt of not doing well in one class and the pride of doing well in others guided *his* decisions about studying.

If you are facing bigger issues with your tween such as drinking, drug use, gang participation, promiscuity, truancy, or other extreme activities, or if you have mental health concerns, you must intervene or seek the help you need to do so.

CHAPTER TWENTY-EIGHT

ENFORCING BOUNDARIES

Once we understand the reason for a boundary, we create a story for it along with a plan to establish and enforce it. I call this our campaign. As you develop it, remember to honor your tween's point of view and leave room for them to weigh in as you firmly set the boundary.

Develop a Campaign

Here are the elements to include in your campaign:

- Definition of the boundary.
- Why it matters (the family value behind the boundary).
- Where it will lead.
- Who it will impact.
- How our tween will "win" by having the boundary.

It may sound something like this:

"We've noticed your screen time is out of control. We want you to enjoy your games. We see that you are learning and getting better at them, and we know it's how you connect with friends. But we also know too much screen time is not good for your brain development, your physical health, or your schoolwork. So we have to find a way to give you screen time but also take care of your brain and allow time for other activities. We talked about different options and have decided we want to start by giving you one hour of screen time a day for two weeks. After two weeks, we will sit down with you again and talk about what is working and what isn't working. We will take into account other things you are doing with your time, how well you are able to transition from screens to other activities, and if you are getting enough time during one session to achieve your goals in your games. What questions do you have? There is one part of this we have not yet decided on, and maybe you can give us your opinion."

Create a Tagline

A tagline is a shortcut to communicate a boundary and the value and campaign behind it. We use it after we have had the longer conversation. It brings us back to this conversation. It also gives us a language known just to us, something we unite on as a family that adds to the glue that holds us together. Good taglines live on the tip of our tongue. They become family mantras.

Here's an example: When my son went through his lying stage, I told him, "Lying changes everything." We went over *The Boy Who Cried Wolf!* I explained that if I couldn't believe what he told me was true, I had to wonder about *everything* he said. This meant that, ultimately, I couldn't trust him. If I could not trust him, I would give him fewer opportunities, less independence.

After that, whenever he lied to me or I suspected he was lying, I asked him if he was telling the truth because "Lying changes everything." I didn't lecture or explain the concept again; we had an understanding. Years later, while talking on the phone, I incorrectly quoted our line. My son corrected me. It stuck! Did he ever lie to me again? Yes, he did. But he also felt what it was like to sit down and have a hard conversation about lying with his mom and dad, which led to moments, prompted by the tagline, when he checked in with himself about lying. The tagline made him feel part of a family that didn't lie, a family that valued honesty. Over time, honesty won.

Taglines

- *Adversity makes us stronger.* (When they have to do something they don't want to and feel discomfort.)
- *Own your part.* (You've done this before and we've talked about your responsibility in this, so I'm going to give you a few moments to consider what you did then tell me what you think.)
- *Breathe through it.* (When anyone in our family gets in the red zone, we try to breathe through it rather than blow fire at one another.)
- *Take it in.* (We all have to be able to take feedback from one another and think about it.)
- *It's okay to be* (tired, hungry, …).
- *Everything's an opportunity.* (A reminder to view all sides of a situation, especially when things haven't gone your way. There is nearly always a plus in it.)
- *Wait for the pause.* (Instead of interrupting me in the middle of a conversation with someone else, including the other parent, *wait for the pause!*)

Communicate the Boundary

Once we decide on a boundary and the consequence for violating it and we've developed our campaign, we discuss it with our tween in a firm, matter-of-fact way at a time when things are calm, precisely when most parents choose *not* to have the conversation. We often think, *Things are going well, I don't want to wreck that,* so we put it off until, inevitably, it explodes from us in a heated moment. This never ends well. Our tween must know our expectations in advance of any breach.

When we impose a boundary in anger, as a way to feel better about ourselves or because we are frustrated, the boundary takes on a different meaning to our tween: Instead of *You are trying to keep me safe*, or *You care about me and this will help me grow*, our tween thinks: *You're on a power trip and you're punishing me*, or hears *You do this and it's wrong!* or *I can't stand it when you do this, so stop it!* even though that is not our intent.

So we must find that settled moment and talk. Calibrate our tone of voice and make eye contact to create an open, non-threatening atmosphere. Chances are we will still get pushback. We must be present. Listen to our tween's protest, make sure they know we hear them and understand their concerns. When we listen, they will calm down. Conversely, when we raise our voice or discount what they're saying mid-sentence with something along the lines of "That's ridiculous!" they will get agitated.

Periodically we should sit with our tween to take stock. Perhaps a boundary needs some loosening up or revising, or our tween deserves recognition for handling one really well. Or possibly, we weren't strong enough with a boundary at the outset, our tween found a workaround, and we need to discuss tightening it up. Nothing is set in stone unless it's working, and we can never assume this without conversation with our tween.

How to Handle "I. Don't. Care."

You drop the bomb—"You've been online an hour longer than we agreed. Screen off. Now. And no screens until tomorrow night." Your tween spits back, "Fine. I don't care." How often have you heard that?! Not to worry. They're mad, and it's a defensive, reactive comment. We don't care if they care. Remember, we are not imposing a consequence for them to care. We're doing it because our family believes that they need limited screen time for the health and wellness of their brain. And so whether they care or not, this is the consequence. We aren't trying to hurt them. It's not a punishment. It's a consequence.

However, we don't modify boundaries because of our tween's argument, but we can take their feedback into account for future reference and let them know we understand their position.

Beware the Pal Syndrome

One of the biggest mistakes we make as parents, as well-intended as it might be, is when we focus on being pals with our tween and withhold the hammer in the interest of our "friendship" with them. Certainly, we want to bond, to be authentic and close. But we must also be willing to be the grown-up in the room, to have the difficult conversations, to create, communicate, and enforce the boundaries that reinforce our family value system, keep our tween safe, and give them the ability to make life-giving choices for themselves. They won't know it, but if friendship with our tween is our aim during these years, we will confuse them and ultimately make them feel untethered, unprotected, aimless. And it will leave us with little or no path when there are boundaries that must be enforced.

When the Bough Breaks

When a boundary is breached, consequences need to be enforced immediately and clearly. Delaying won't work. When we wait, we lose the force of the consequence. It's the difference between "You've been on the computer too long. You're going to have to shut if off for the rest of the night" and "You've been at it too long. Starting Monday, you're off for a week."

Simply stating the boundary will fall on deaf ears. Some parents will complain their tween is violating a boundary and nag at them to mind, but they never really enforce it. For example, a parent says, "Get off the screen." Ten minutes later they say, "I told you to get off the screen!" Five minutes later, they say, "If you don't get off the screen, we are going to have problems!" Ten minutes later they say, "You are supposed to be off the screens!" In this case, the parent is exerting so. much. energy! They probably feel frustrated and taken advantage of, but they are nowhere near their desired outcome because they have not *enforced* the consequence.

If we want our boundaries to succeed, consistency and follow-through are also key. We are showing that if we believe in something, we *will* stick to it, and we will follow through with consequences when our tween violates a boundary—*every time*. No matter what. Dads back up moms. Moms back up dads. The boundary is always the boundary, no negotiation, no next time, no "I'll count to three" then nothing. That's why we want to be careful with how many boundaries we set: The follow-through can be tough.

Why Consistency and Follow-Through Can Be Hard

It takes work, which can be really difficult when we are tired, we know it's going to be a fight, or we are happy and having fun with our tween. Plus, we have to implement boundaries, be consistent, and follow through as situations arise, which could be any time, convenient or not. Last, we must also remember what we said when we set the boundary. Our tween will not miss a chance to twist our words. Rest assured, though, God stands by with a ready assist for strength if we let Him in and remember to ask for it.

With strong boundaries, consistency, and follow-through, things can be much less dramatic—at least on our end…a sort of *I'm not mad at you, I don't have to strongarm you, I am simply letting you know the boundary has been reached*. Think of the difference between "Your time is up. Get off the iPad!" versus "How much longer until that segment is over? Five minutes? Okay, let that be the end of your time then." The first begs to be blown off and opens the door for an argument. The latter invites our tween to work with us.

As with when we are setting boundaries, we will get pushback when we enforce them, no matter how strong our emotional connection or calm our approach. It's the nature of the tween years. But we don't have to engage in every comment. In fact, not engaging will often reduce the time our tween spends pushing back.

Power Struggles: When the Fuse Blows

Brandon has been on screens all day—TikTok, YouTube, sports on TV. Now he's playing video games. His mom tells him it's time to stop. He asks for five more minutes; ten minutes later, he is still playing. She asks him again. "Why?" he says. "Just let me have another few minutes!" He starts shouting and name calling. His mother wants to yell back, take away screens until further notice. Instead, standing next to him, she says, in a calm voice, "It's time to hand over the controller." Brandon rolls his eyes, howls and complains his parents are unfair. Mom counts silently to five and then says, "I am waiting for the controller. It's time to end. You have to move onto something else—walk the dog, help your dad outside in the yard, help me in the kitchen. I get you are disappointed and want more time, but that more time is not right now." While Brandon complains and throws his controller, his mother waits without speaking. She wants to tell him his behavior is unacceptable, and he should be embarrassed by it. She is angry and offended when he acts this way. It takes every ounce of self-control not to lunge across the room and yell at him. But this would only escalate the situation. Eventually, she calmly walks to where he has thrown the remote, picks it up, thanks him, and walks away to put it where it is stored. Like most kids, Brandon will carry on about how unfair things are in his house. Later, when he is calmer, she will address his behavior.

When we do engage, we must remember to pace the conversation, slowing it down by letting our tween talk, giving them the chance to burn their energy. We must work to keep emotions under 5 on the scale I described to you in Part Six: I See You. Remember: If you see the discussion crossing the bridge, take a bathroom break, get something to drink, or let your tween know the discussion is ending for now with something like, "I'm glad we talked about this. Let's come back to it tonight/tomorrow at (specific time)." Just be sure to value their disappointment. It makes sense they are unhappy with your decision and follow-through.

Here are some examples of what follow-through looks like:

- Our tween swore at us: "In the spirit of owning your part, please think about what you just said and see if there is a better way you can say that. If not, then I don't have an answer to your question. As I've said to you before, swearing does not get you a conversation with me."
- Our tween lied about where they were and shut down when confronted with it: "I've told you lying changes everything, and now that you have lied again, I have a hard time trusting where you say you were. What is really going on here? It seems like you're not ready to talk about it, so you're going to have to take a week off from (seeing that friend/going to town) until we can build back some trust."
- Our tween lost their temper; we let them cool off and return to the conversation: "Earlier, you got really angry and were not able to breathe through it. Talk to me about what happened, because that is scary and hurtful to the rest of us to watch you in that kind of pain. Can you think of ways you might handle those big feelings differently?"

Notice that in each of these examples, we are following through on limits we had set in previous conversations with our tween. Follow-through can be reinforcing a tagline (which, by the way, may take a while to stick so be patient) or taking away a privilege. It can be inviting conversation—giving our tween a chance to own their behavior, or tabling the conversation until our tween calms down. (Just because our tween wants something now does not mean they get it now! That's not the way the world works.)

Co-parenting and Setting Boundaries

When co-parenting, it is ideal to work together to set similar boundaries, to create a consistent message your tween can count on. This won't always happen, but know that the more boundaries differ between co-parents, the harder it is for a tween to interpret the boundaries and transition from one home to the other.

A Final Word on Boundaries

As you face the challenge of setting and enforcing boundaries, remember, properly applied, they are acts of love. Without them, we cannot achieve full emotional connection with our tween. They teach discipline, delayed gratification, tolerance, and so much more. When we involve our tween in the boundaries we set for them and put the onus on them to make the right decision, they own the boundary and the consequence if they violate it, engraining the lessons we intend for them. When they understand that boundaries enforce family values and we are consistent and follow through in applying them, they feel safe, which gives them confidence to meet the world, take healthy risks, and grow.

What's more, as we know from Part Two: It's Not You, It's Neuroscience, the tween years are a time of explosive neural pathway growth. For better or worse, the behavior and emotions they experience most often during their tween years are being coded into their brains. We want to lock in what it feels like to push a boundary and suffer a consequence and also what it feels like to respect a boundary. So stick with it. Show your love. Drop the hammer when you must.

QUESTIONS TO PONDER

1. What two boundaries are most important to you?

2. In what situations do you allow for natural consequences? What comes up for you when you let them happen?

3. Can you think of a boundary that is important to you and run it through the "campaign"? What is the sentence that describes it, the larger conversation that explains it, and a tagline you can use to reference it going forward?

4. Do you ever say you're going to enforce a consequence but lack follow-through?

5. If you're in a divorce situation, what boundaries are the same between both homes? What issues are hard to parent together?

CONCLUSION

On the Side of Us

Putting It All Together

"I define connection as the energy that exists between people
when they feel seen, heard and valued; when they can give
and receive without judgment; and when they derive
sustenance and strength from the relationship."

—BRENÉ BROWN, PHD, RESEARCH PROFESSOR, LECTURER, AUTHOR

"Above all, keep loving one another earnestly,
since love covers a multitude of sins."

—1 PETER 4:8 ESV

As I finish writing this book, my son turns twelve years old. We went for his annual appointment with the pediatrician, and although he hasn't reached stage one of puberty (no hair in new places), he definitely looks miles away from the little nine-year-old boy of just three years ago. Now, he meets friends in town by himself. He's riding his bike all over our community with his close friends. He has a large football team that he sees as his support system. He can't get enough of the sport, or baseball either. He has text message groups that include boys and girls.

I am not as welcomed as I once was. Yet he wants to do well, and he looks to us—my husband and me—for reassurance. I can see him sneaking into the teen years. Just yesterday, he went out on his bike and, for the very first time, he was late for curfew. I told him he was an hour late, and he was surprised himself. You see, it's the first time he was out and not counting on us to pick him up. He had never really been anywhere without an adult or a plan that one would give him a ride home at a particular time. His bike gives him new freedom.

When he was maybe four years old, he said to me, "Mom, I love you so much it hurts." Today, I feel that. I grieve the loss of the child that he was as I watch him move into his teen years. I can get teary and heart heavy. Writing this book as I raised him through his tween years was a huge benefit. My biggest takeaways, the things it reinforced most for me, were:

1. *Really* listen. I asked him questions to get a sense of what it is like for him to meander in the world. More times than I could ever count, my kneejerk inclination was to get up and multitask during our conversations. I had to work hard to let this pass, and stay 100 percent focused on what he was saying and doing.

2. Emotional awareness. There were numerous times when he would yell, swear at us, or throw something. I wanted to match his intensity and shout back at him not to behave that way. Of course, when I did, it didn't help. I practiced going back to him later, when things were calmer, with a firm but gentle, "That is not acceptable," then asked what he noticed about himself when

he was raging. Sometimes he would talk about it and sometimes he wouldn't. To get him to open up, I used our two taglines a lot: *"What was coming up for you?"* and *"Know it. Say it."* Because if we know what we're thinking and can verbalize it, we can figure out what to do about it.

3. **Loosen the rope.** I marvel at watching my son love football: the excitement in his voice when he talks about it. I feel pride watching him get his uniform all set the night before a game or practice, and it shows up in my behavior toward him: He feels my acceptance and validation that he is doing well. Do I worry he will get hurt playing and think it wasn't worth it? Of course! But I let go so that he can experience life in a way that makes sense for him. And that applies to the rest of his life: He has to find his friend group. He has to study (or not) for quizzes and tests and see how he does. He has to practice his viola in his way, go out in public without me, and get feedback from other adults. I cannot watch over him all of the time nor can I choreograph his every move. It wouldn't be him. It would not serve him long term.

4. **Set those boundaries and follow through.** In our house, you can't put little effort into schoolwork, come home with a low grade, and expect no conversation. We *will* talk about it; we will not let the moment pass in the hope that next time will be better. You will feel the rope tug you back on course. We have a boundary here: "If you get under a certain grade, you will have a scheduled study period with me or Dad until your next test"…and we will follow through. Even when I was tired, I've had to say things I knew would irritate my son. And follow through. Boundaries matter.

I start each morning with Scripture. I've been doing this for the past several years, and it gives me a focus, a grounding during the day when I struggle. It also gives me a sense of peace and strength. It has helped me with my parenting in all the ways I've discussed in the book. Maybe the Bible isn't your thing, but find what is. How can you start your day in a way that grounds you and gives you strength?

At the close of this book, I also wonder what people will think, how the book will sell, what my publishers will want to change. All of this insecurity could stop me in my tracks. It brings up the soil issues I experienced as a student, the struggles I had with the written word. I still think of myself as a bad writer, even after all these years—hundreds of college papers, a dissertation, and writing a book. I've had to calm that inner child and remind her I have learned to write and I actually enjoy it now. Soil issues are at the base of all of us. It's what we do with them that is most important.

Would I rather follow the nudge to help my fellow parents, write this book, and put it out there, or cave to my issues and shelve it, keeping all it contains a quiet secret? In the same way, we cannot let our soil issues, or the inevitable mistakes we all make, keep us from being the parents we are capable of becoming, of building the emotional connection available to all of us.

Lucky me: I have a five-year-old, and in just a few short years she will be a tween and I will be asking, "Who are you and what have you done with my kid?" I'll start the process of parenting a tween all over. I can already tell it's going to be a very different experience: not only because she's a girl but also because her personality is nothing like her brother's. I'll make more mistakes, and then I'll hit home runs. Every child is different, so most likely what I get wrong and what I get right will be different. Each journey is unique to each child. But the guideposts along the way are the same:

- Tween brains are changing—dramatically.
- Tweens experience emotions they do not recognize.
- Tweens are socially awkward.
- Tweens don't know how to communicate any of this…and they don't know that they don't know.

So, equipped with our love for our tween, we set out:

- To see them.
- To know them.
- To be there for them.
- To keep them safe.

It's the journey that matters...because it is the journey that amounts to our relationship with our tween, and we are in it together. I hope with all I've shared, you find your way to the route that exists uniquely for you and your child.

ACKNOWLEDGMENTS

First and foremost, I thank God. The initial draft of this book poured from me like some out-of-body experience with no direction or force from me. Rather, it came by way of something bigger, deeper, and more soulful. To me, it was the Holy Spirit, and I believe it is inside every one of us. If we let it, it will guide us to good, amazing, hard, and wonderful things. Thanks be to God.

I am thankful also to my parents, who pushed the importance of education. It was while finishing my master's degree the idea for this book came to me. I wanted to offer parents a path to express love and care for their tweens in a way that could build their resilience and confidence to take on the world.

Fast forward twenty years from that first thought: I shared my long-lost vision with my mother-in-law, Nancy Craig. She encouraged me to pick up my pen and keep writing. Every conversation, she asked me how it was going, and she read and made edits to numerous early drafts. I am so thankful she believed in my ability and pushed me to bring my vision to life.

My amazing mentor Beth Fagin was one of the first people to read an early draft of my book. She was so supportive and kept me going. Thank you, Beth, for caring and always being there for me.

My sister-in-law took time from raising her own two tweens to read an early version of the manuscript and offered encouraging words, reiterating the necessity of this book. Thank you, Bethany Craig, for taking time to read, reflect, and share in my vision.

Without my husband, Douglas Craig, to watch the kids, lean on when I was unsure, talk through complicated concepts, and bounce ideas off, I would not have had the hours upon hours to write and bring this book to life. I am thankful for a partner who believes my project should see light and who was willing to invest so much time and effort to support it.

My kids, Livvy and Owen, sacrificed for this book. There were weekends they didn't see me because I was writing, editing, or meeting with my editor. They were so loving and caring toward me. Somehow they knew this book mattered and they were behind it. I am grateful to them.

This book could not have been organized and presented as it is without the word crafting and meticulous editing from Pamela Dey Vossler. She is sharp-minded, good humored, and a gifted writer who worked hard to capture my voice. She joined me after those early first drafts and has been with me every step of the way since. She brought me to my agent and helped me synthesize my knowledge and experience into the manuscript. As the author of this book, I could have asked for no better translator. We worked on proposals to potential publishers and completed the manuscript before it had even sold. She put in more hours than I can imagine and never faltered in her belief in me and this book. To have her invest so wholly in something so important to me has been humbling.

I thank my agent, Rick Richter of Aevitas Creative Management. He took a chance on a no-name author with no social media following, supported us through numerous publisher passes, and encouraged us to keep trying. I would not be here without him.

To the publisher that said, "Yes!" and brought this book to life—Worthy, a division of Hachette Book Group: Thank you! Thank you! Thank you!

I am grateful to all the people who shared a conversation, a resource, an idea; helped me network, looked at a part of the book, encouraged me to write, shared their stories with me, especially Liam McDonough, Krista Carnes, Wendy Ward, Jen Faye Colombo, and Marina Shapiro.

I have worked with so many absolutely amazing people in my office over the past two decades. From them, I have learned so much about love, humanity, healing, and resiliency. Thank you to every last one of you for sharing your life story with me, for trusting me, and adding to the inspiration that has become this book.

ABOUT THE AUTHOR

Amanda Craig, PhD, is a Licensed Marriage and Family Therapist (LMFT) based in southern Connecticut and New York City. A native of Richfield, Minnesota, Dr. Craig has been in practice for more than twenty years. She has worked with children, adolescents, adults, couples, and families in a variety of settings including research departments, juvenile corrections facilities, high schools, Fortune 500 companies, substance abuse programs, and university/college classrooms, as well as private practice. She specializes in treating relationship issues such as communication, conflict resolution, and infidelity as well as individual depression, anxiety, addiction, and life–work harmony. Three things she knows for sure: 1) We are not defined by adversities, but how we handle them. 2) Taking healthy risks, setting boundaries, and stepping outside our comfort zone will bring fulfillment in life and relationships. 3) Make the most of this day, whatever that means to you, whatever you can do, no matter how small it seems.

Dr. Craig lives in Darien, Connecticut, with her husband, five-year-old daughter, twelve-year-old son, ten chickens, one dog, two cats, and two fish.